Functional Programming for
Java Developers

Functional Programming for Java Developers

Dean Wampler

Beijing · Cambridge · Farnham · Köln · Sebastopol · Tokyo

Functional Programming for Java Developers
by Dean Wampler

Published by O'Reilly Media, Inc., 1005 Gravenstein Highway North, Sebastopol, CA 95472.

O'Reilly books may be purchased for educational, business, or sales promotional use. Online editions are also available for most titles (*http://my.safaribooksonline.com*). For more information, contact our corporate/institutional sales department: (800) 998-9938 or *corporate@oreilly.com*.

Editors: Mike Loukides and Shawn Wallace		**Cover Designer:** Karen Montgomery	
Production Editor: Teresa Elsey		**Interior Designer:** David Futato	
		Illustrator: Robert Romano	

Printing History:

July 2011:   First Edition.

ISBN: 978-1-449-31103-2

[LSI]

1312392351

Table of Contents

Preface

Welcome to Functional Programming for Java Developers

Why should a Java developer learn about functional programming (FP)? After all, hasn't functional programming been safely hidden in academia for decades? Isn't object-oriented programming (OOP) all we really need? This book explains why functional programming has become an important tool for the challenges of our time and how you, a Java developer, can use it to your advantage.

The recent interest in functional programming started as a response to the growing pervasiveness of *concurrency* as a way of scaling horizontally, through *parallelism*. Multithreaded programming (see, e.g., [Goetz2006]) is difficult to do well and few developers are good at it. As we'll see, functional programming offers better strategies for writing robust, concurrent software.

An example of the greater need for horizontal scalability is the growth of massive data sets requiring management and analysis, the so-called *big data* trend. These are data sets that are too large for traditional database management systems. They require clusters of computers to store and process the data. Today, it's not just Google, Yahoo!, Facebook, and Twitter who work with big data. Many organizations face this challenge.

Once you learn the benefits of functional programming, you find that it improves all the code you write. When I learned functional programming a few years ago, it re-energized my enthusiasm for programming. I saw new, exciting ways to approach old problems. The rigor of functional programming complemented the design and testing benefits of *test-driven development*, giving me greater confidence in my work. I learned functional programming using the Scala programming language [Scala] and co-wrote a book on Scala with Alex Payne, called *Programming Scala* (O'Reilly). Scala is a JVM language, a potential successor to Java, with the goal of bringing object-oriented and functional programming into one coherent whole. Clojure is the other well-known functional language on the JVM. It is a Lisp dialect that minimizes the use of OOP in favor of functional programming. Clojure embodies a powerful vision for how programming should be done.

Fortunately, you don't have to adopt a new language to enjoy many of the benefits of functional programming. Back in early 1990s, I used an object-oriented approach in the C software I wrote, until I could use C++. Similarly, if you're working with an object-oriented language, like Java, you can still apply many of the ideas from functional programming.

Unfortunately, much of the literature on functional programming is difficult to understand for people who are new to it. This short book offers a pragmatic, approachable introduction to functional programming. While aimed at the Java developer, the principles are general and will benefit anyone familiar with an object-oriented language.

I assume that you are well versed in object-oriented programming and you can read Java code. You'll find some exercises at the end of each chapter to help you practice and expand on what you've learned.

Because this is a short introduction and because it is difficult to represent some functional concepts in Java, there will be several topics that I won't discuss in the text, although I have added glossary entries, for completeness. These topics include *currying*, *partial application*, and *comprehensions*. I'll briefly discuss several other topics, such as *combinators*, *laziness*, and *monads*, to give you a taste of their importance. However, fully understanding these topics isn't necessary when you're new to functional programming.

I hope you find functional programming as seductive as I did. Let me know how it goes!

You can learn more at the book's catalog page (*http://oreilly.com/catalog/9781449311032/*).

Conventions Used in This Book

The following typographical conventions are used in this book:

Italic
> Indicates new terms, URLs, email addresses, filenames, and file extensions. Many italicized terms are defined in the Glossary.

`Constant width`
> Used for program listings, as well as within paragraphs to refer to program elements such as variable or function names, databases, data types, environment variables, statements, and keywords.

`Constant width bold`
> Shows commands or other text that should be typed literally by the user.

`Constant width italic`
> Shows text that should be replaced with user-supplied values or by values determined by context.

This icon signifies a tip, suggestion, or general note.

 This icon indicates a warning or caution.

Using the Code Examples

This book is here to help you get your job done. In general, you may use the code in this book in your programs and documentation. You do not need to contact us for permission unless you're reproducing a significant portion of the code. For example, writing a program that uses several chunks of code from this book does not require permission. Selling or distributing a CD-ROM of examples from O'Reilly books does require permission. Answering a question by citing this book and quoting example code does not require permission. Incorporating a significant amount of example code from this book into your product's documentation does require permission.

We appreciate, but do not require, attribution. An attribution usually includes the title, author, publisher, and ISBN. For example: "*Functional Programming for Java Developers*, by Dean Wampler (O'Reilly). Copyright 2011 Dean Wampler, 978-1-449-31103-2."

If you feel your use of code examples falls outside fair use or the permission given above, feel free to contact us at permissions@oreilly.com (*mailto:permissions@oreilly.com*).

Some of the code examples were adapted from examples provided with the Akka distribution, copyright © 2009-2011 Scalable Solutions AB. The Akka code base is covered by the Apache 2 License.

Getting the Code Examples

You can download the code examples from *http://examples.oreilly.com/ 9781449311032/*. Unzip the files to a convenient location. See the README file in the distribution for instructions on building and using the examples.

Note that some of the files won't actually compile, because they introduce speculative concepts that aren't supported by current compilers or libraries. Those files end with the extension .javax. (The build process skips them.)

Safari® Books Online

Safari Books Online is an on-demand digital library that lets you easily search over 7,500 technology and creative reference books and videos to find the answers you need quickly.

With a subscription, you can read any page and watch any video from our library online. Read books on your cell phone and mobile devices. Access new titles before they are available for print, and get exclusive access to manuscripts in development and post feedback for the authors. Copy and paste code samples, organize your favorites, download chapters, bookmark key sections, create notes, print out pages, and benefit from tons of other time-saving features.

O'Reilly Media has uploaded this book to the Safari Books Online service. To have full digital access to this book and others on similar topics from O'Reilly and other publishers, sign up for free at *http://my.safaribooksonline.com*.

How to Contact Us

Please address comments and questions concerning this book to the publisher:

O'Reilly Media, Inc.
1005 Gravenstein Highway North
Sebastopol, CA 95472
800-998-9938 (in the United States or Canada)
707-829-0515 (international or local)
707-829-0104 (fax)

We have a web page for this book, where we list errata, examples, and any additional information. You can access this page at:

http://oreilly.com/catalog/0636920021667/

To comment or ask technical questions about this book, send email to:

bookquestions@oreilly.com

For more information about our books, courses, conferences, and news, see our website at *http://www.oreilly.com*.

Find us on Facebook: *http://facebook.com/oreilly*

Follow us on Twitter: *http://twitter.com/oreillymedia*

Watch us on YouTube: *http://www.youtube.com/oreillymedia*

Acknowledgments

I want to think my editor at O'Reilly, Mike Loukides, who suggested that I write this book. Brendan McNichols and Bobby Norton provided helpful feedback on drafts of the book. Debasish Ghosh provided valuable comments on the Liskov Substitution Principle and suggested the Olin Shivers quotes on the meaning of `foldLeft` and `foldRight` [Shivers]. Daniel Spiewak provided invaluable feedback that helped clarify many of the concepts in the book, such as Monads.

I have learned a lot about functional programming from fellow developers around the world, many of whom are fellow Scala enthusiasts. Martin Odersky, Jonas Bonér, Debasish Ghosh, James Iry, Daniel Spiewak, Simon Peyton Jones, Rich Hickey, Conal Elliot, David Pollak, Paul Snively, and others have illuminated dark corners with their writing, speaking, personal conversations, and code! Finally, my fellow members of the Chicago Area Scala Enthusiasts (CASE) group have also been a source of valuable feedback and inspiration over the last several years.

Of course, any errors and omissions are mine alone.

CHAPTER 1

Why Functional Programming?

A few years ago, when many developers started talking about functional programming (FP) as the best way to approach *concurrency*, I decided it was time to learn more and judge for myself. I expected to learn some new ideas, but I assumed I would still use object-oriented programming (OOP) as my primary approach to software development. I was wrong.

As I learned about functional programming, I found good ideas for implementing concurrency, as I expected, but I also found that it brought new *clarity* to my thinking about the design of types* and functions. It also allowed me to write more *concise* code. Functional programming made me rethink where module boundaries should go and how to make those modules better for reuse. I found that the functional programming community was building innovative and more powerful type systems that help enforce correctness. I also concluded that functional programming is a better fit for many of the unique challenges of our time, like working with massive data sets and remaining *agile* as requirements change ever more rapidly and schedules grow ever shorter.

Instead of remaining an OOP developer who tosses in some FP for seasoning, today I write functional programs that use objects judiciously. You could say that I came to FP for the concurrency, but I stayed for the "paradigm shift."

The funny thing is, we've been here before. A very similar phenomenon occurred in the 80s when OOP began to go mainstream. Objects are an ideal way of representing graphical widgets, so OOP was a natural fit for developing Graphical User Interfaces (GUIs). However, once people started using objects, they found them to be an intuitive way to represent many "domains." You could model the problem domain in objects, then put the *same object model* in the code! Even implementation details, like various forms of input and output, seemed ideal for object modeling.

But let's be clear, both FP and OOP are tools, not panaceas. Each has advantages and disadvantages. It's easy to stick with the tried and true, even when there might be a better way available. Even so, it's hard to believe that objects, which have worked so

---

* I'll occasionally use *type* and *class* interchangeably, but they aren't synonyms. See the definitions in Glossary.

well in the past, could be any less valuable today, isn't it? For me, my growing interest in functional programming isn't a repudiation of objects, which have proven benefits. Rather, it's a recognition that the drawbacks of objects are harder to ignore when faced with the programming challenges of today. The times are different than they were when objects were ascendant several decades ago.

Here, in brief, is why I became a functional programmer and why I believe you should learn about it, too. For me, functional programming offers the best approach to meet the following challenges, which I face every day.

I Have to Be Good at Writing Concurrent Programs

It used to be that a few of the "smart guys" on the team wrote most of the concurrent code, using multithreaded concurrency, which requires carefully synchronized access to shared, mutable state. Occasionally everyone would get a midnight call to debug some nasty concurrency bug that appeared in production. But most of the time, most of the developers could ignore concurrency.

Today, even your phone has several CPU cores (or your next one will). Learning how to write robust concurrent software is no longer optional. Fortunately, functional programming gives you the right principles to think about concurrency and it has spawned several higher-level concurrency abstractions that make the job far easier.

 Multithreaded programming, requiring synchronized access to shared, *mutable* state, is the *assembly language of concurrency*.

Most Programs Are Just Data Management Problems

I work a lot with *big data* these days, mostly using the Apache Hadoop ecosystem of tools, built around *MapReduce* [Hadoop]. When you are ingesting *terabytes* of new data *each day*, when you need to cleanse and store that data, then do analysis on the *petabytes* of accumulated data, you simply can't afford the overhead of objects. You want very efficient data structures and operations on that data, with minimal overhead. The old *agile* catch phrase, *What's the simplest thing that could possibly work?*, takes on new meaning.

I started thinking about how we manage smaller data sets, say in a typical IT application backed by a database. If objects add overhead for big data problems, what about the overhead for smaller data problems? Performance and storage size are less likely to be issues in this case, but team agility *is* a pervasive issue. How does a small team remain nimble when enhancing an IT application, year after year? How does the team keep the code base as concise as possible?

I've come to believe that faithfully representing the domain object model in code should be questioned. *Object-relational mapping* (ORM) and similar forms of object middleware add overhead for transforming relational data into objects, moving those objects around the application, then ultimately transforming them back to relational data for updates. Of course, all this extra code has to be tested and maintained.

I know this practice arose in part because we love objects and we often hate relational data, or maybe we just hate working with relational databases. (I speak from personal experience.) However, relational data, such as the result sets for queries, are really just collections that can be manipulated in a functional way. Would it be better to work directly with that data?

I'll show you how working directly with more fundamental collections of data minimizes the overhead of working with object models, while still avoiding duplication and promoting reuse.

Functional Programming Is More Modular

Years ago, I had a large client that struggled to get work done with their bloated code base. Their competition was running circles around them. One day I saw something that captured their problems in a nutshell. I walked by a five-foot partition wall with a UML diagram that covered the wall. I remember one class in particular, a `Customer` class. It stretched the whole five feet. This was a failure of modularity, specifically in finding the correct levels of abstraction and decomposition. The `Customer` class had become a grab bag of everything anyone might associate with one of their customers.

In the late 1980s, when object-oriented programming was on the rise, many people hoped that objects would finally solve the problem of building reusable components that you plug together to build applications, greatly reducing costs and development times. This vision seems so reasonable that it is easy to overlook the fact that it didn't turn out as well as we hoped. Most of the successful examples of reusable libraries are platforms that defined their own standards that everyone had to follow. Examples include the JDK, the Spring Framework, and the Eclipse plugin API. Even most of the third-party "component libraries" we might use (for example, Apache Commons) have their own custom APIs that we must conform to. For the rest of the code we need, we still rewrite a lot of it project after project. Hence, object-oriented software development isn't the "component assembly" we hoped would emerge.

The nearly limitless flexibility of objects actually undermines the potential for reuse, because there are few standards for how objects should interconnect and we can't agree on even basic names of things! Systems with greater constraints are actually more modular, which is a paradox. The book *Design Rules: The Power of Modularity* [Baldwin2000] demonstrates that the explosive growth of the PC industry was made possible when IBM created a de facto standard for the personal computer hardware architecture. Because of standardized buses for peripherals and connectors, it enabled innovators to create new, better, and cheaper drives, mice, monitors, motherboards, etc. Digital electronics is itself a great example of a modular system. Each wire carries only a 0 or 1 signal, yet when you join them together in groups of 8, 16, 32, and 64, you can build up protocol layers that make possible all the wonderful things that we've come to do with computers.

There are no similar standards for object-based components. Various attempts like CORBA and COM had modest success, but ultimately failed for the same basic reasons, that objects are at the wrong level of abstraction. Concepts like "customer" are rarely new, yet we can't find a way to stop inventing a new representation for them in every new project, because each project brings its own context and requirements.

However, if we notice that an object is fundamentally just an aggregation of data, then we can see a way to define better standardized abstractions at lower levels than objects, analogous to digit circuits. These standards are the fundamental collections like *list*, *map*, and *set*, along with "primitive" types like numbers and few well-defined domain concepts (e.g., Money in a financial application).

A further aid to modularity is the nature of *functions* in functional programming, which avoid side effects, making them free of dependencies on other objects and therefore easier to reuse in many contexts.

The net result is that a functional program defines abstractions where they are more useful, easier to reuse, compose, and also test.

 Any arbitrarily complex object can be decomposed into "atomic" values (like primitives) and collections containing those values and other collections.

I Have to Work Faster and Faster

Development cycles are going asymptotically to zero length. That sounds crazy, especially if you started professional programming when I did, when projects typically lasted months, even years. However, today there are plenty of Internet sites that deploy new code *several times a day* and all of us are feeling the pressure to get work done more quickly, without sacrificing quality, of course.

When schedules were longer, it made more sense to model your domain carefully and to *implement* that domain in code. If you made a mistake, it would take months to correct with a new release. Today, for most projects, understanding the domain precisely is less important than delivering some value quickly. Our understanding of the domain will change rapidly anyway, as we and our customers discover new insights with each deployment. If we misunderstand some aspect of the domain, we can fix those mistakes quickly when we do frequent deployments.

If careful modeling seems less important, faithfully *implementing* the object model is even more suspect today than before. While Agile Software Development has greatly improved our quality and our ability to respond to change, we need to rethink ways to keep our code "minimally sufficient" for the requirements today, yet flexible for change. Functional programming helps us do just that.

Functional Programming Is a Return to Simplicity

Finally, building on the previous points, I see functional programming as a reaction against accidental complexity, the kind we add ourselves by our implementation choices, as opposed to the inherent complexity of the problem domain.[†] So, for example, much of the object-oriented middleware in our applications today is unnecessary and wasteful, in my opinion.

I know that some of these claims are provocative. I'm not trying to convince you to abandon objects altogether or to become an FP zealot. I'm trying to give you a bigger toolbox and a broadened perspective, so you can make more informed design choices and maybe refresh your enthusiasm for the art and science of software development. I hope this short introduction will show you why my thinking changed. Maybe your thinking will change, too.

Let's begin!

---

† I don't mean that functional programming is *simple*. Becoming an expert in functional programming requires mastery of many advanced, yet powerful concepts.

CHAPTER 2

What Is Functional Programming?

Functional programming, in its "purest" sense, is rooted in how functions, variables, and values actually work in mathematics, which is different from how they typically work in most programming languages.

Functional programming got its start before digital computers even existed. Many of the theoretical underpinnings of computation were developed in the 1930s by mathematicians like Alonzo Church and Haskell Curry.

In the 1930s, Alonzo Church developed the Lambda Calculus, which is a formalism for defining and invoking functions (called *applying* them). Today, the syntax and behavior of most programming languages reflect this model.

Haskell Curry (for whom the Haskell language is named) helped develop Combinatory Logic, which provides an alternative theoretical basis for computation. Combinatory Logic examines how *combinators*, which are essentially functions, combine to represent a computation. One practical application of combinators is to use them as building blocks for constructing parsers. They are also useful for representing the steps in a planned computation, which can be analyzed for possible bugs and optimization opportunities.

More recently, Category Theory has been a fruitful source of ideas for functional programming, such as ways to structure computations so that side effects like IO (input and output), which change the state of the "world," are cleanly separated from code with no side effects.

A lot of the literature on functional programming reflects its mathematical roots, which can be overwhelming if you don't have a strong math background. In contrast, object-oriented programming seems more intuitive and approachable. Fortunately, you can learn and use the principles of functional programming without a thorough grounding in mathematics.

The first language to incorporate functional programming ideas was Lisp,[*] which was developed in the late 1950s and is the second-oldest high-level programming language, after Fortran. The ML family of programming languages started in the 1970s, including Caml, OCaml (a hybrid object-functional language), and Microsoft's F#. Perhaps the best known functional language that comes closest to functional "purity" is Haskell, which was started in the early 1990s. Other recent functional languages include Clojure and Scala, both of which run on the JVM but are being ported to the .NET environment. Today, many other languages are incorporating ideas from functional programming.

The Basic Principles of Functional Programming

Don't all programming languages have *functions*? If so, why aren't all programming languages considered *functional* languages? Functional languages share a few basic principles.

Avoiding Mutable State

The first principle is the use of *immutable* values. You might recall the famous *Pythagorean equation* from school, which relates the lengths of the sides of a triangle:

$$x^2 + y^2 = z^2$$

If I give you *values* for the *variables* x and y, say x=3 and y=4, you can compute the value for z (5 in this case). The key idea here is that values are *never* modified. It would be crazy to say 3++, but you could start over by assigning *new* values to the *same* variables.

Most programming languages don't make a clear distinction between a value (i.e., the contents of memory) and a variable that refers to it. In Java, we'll use `final` to prohibit *variable* reassignment, so we get objects that are immutable *values*.

Why should we avoid mutating values? First, allowing mutable values is what makes multithreaded programming so difficult. If multiple threads can modify the same shared value, you have to synchronize access to that value. This is quite tedious and error-prone programming that even the experts find challenging [Goetz2006]. If you make a value immutable, the synchronization problem disappears. Concurrent reading is harmless, so multithreaded programming becomes far easier.

A second benefit of immutable values relates to program correctness in other ways. It is harder to understand and exhaustively test code with mutable values, particularly if mutations aren't localized to one place. Some of the most difficult bugs to find in large systems occur when state is modified non-locally, by client code that is located elsewhere in the program.

---

[*] See the References for links to information about the languages mentioned here.

Consider the following example, where a mutable `List` is used to hold a customer's orders:

```
public class Customer {
  // No setter method
  private final List<Order> orders;
  public List<Order> getOrders() { return orders; }
  public Customer(...) {...}
}
```

It's reasonable that clients of `Customer` will want to view the list of `Orders`. Unfortunately, by exposing the list through the getter method, `getOrders`, we've lost control over them! A client could modify the list without our knowledge. We didn't provide a setter for `orders` and it is declared `final`, but these protections only prevent assigning a new list to `orders`. The list itself can still be modified.

We could work around this problem by having `getOrders` return a copy of the list or by adding special accessor methods to `Customer` that provide controlled access to `orders`. However, copying the list is expensive, especially for large lists. Adding ad-hoc accessor methods increases the complexity of the object, the testing burden, and the effort required of other programmers to comprehend and use the class.

However, if the list of orders is immutable and the list elements are immutable, these worries are gone. Clients can call the getter method to read the orders, but they can't modify the orders, so we retain control over the state of the object.

What happens when the list of orders is supposed to change, but it has become huge? Should we relent and make it mutable to avoid the overhead of making big copies? Fortunately, we have an efficient way to copy large data structures; we'll reuse the parts that aren't changing! When we add a new order to our list of orders, we can reuse the rest of the list. We'll explore how in Chapter 3.

Some mutability is unavoidable. All programs have to do IO. Otherwise, they could do nothing but heat up the CPU, as a joke goes. However, functional programming encourages us to think strategically about when and where mutability is necessary. If we encapsulate mutations in well-defined areas and keep the rest of the code free of mutation, we improve the robustness and modularity of our code.

We still need to handle mutations in a thread-safe way. Software Transactional Memory and the Actor Model give us this safety. We'll explore both in Chapter 4.

Make your objects immutable. Declare fields `final`. Only provide getters for fields and then only when necessary. Be careful that mutable `final` objects can still be modified. Use mutable collections carefully. See "Minimize Mutability" in [Bloch2008] for more tips.

Functions as First-Class Values

In Java, we are accustomed to passing objects and primitive values to methods, returning them from methods, and assigning them to variables. This means that objects and primitives are *first-class values* in Java. Note that classes themselves aren't first-class values, although the reflection API offers information about classes.

Functions are not first-class values in Java. Let's clarify the difference between a *method* and a *function*.

 A *method* is a block of code attached to a particular class. It can only be called in the context of the class, if it's defined to be static, or in the context of an instance of the class. A *function* is more general. It is not attached to any particular class or object. Therefore, all instance *methods* are *functions* where one of the arguments is the object.

Java only has methods and methods aren't *first-class* in Java. You can't pass a method as an argument to another method, return a method from a method, or assign a method as a value to a variable.

However, most *anonymous inner classes* are effectively function "wrappers." Many Java methods take an instance of an interface that declares one method. Here's a common example, specifying an ActionListener for an AWT/Swing application (see the Preface for details on obtaining and using all the source code examples in this book):

```
package functions;
import java.awt.*;
import java.awt.event.*;

class HelloButtonApp2 {
        private final Button button = new Button();

    public HelloButtonApp2() {
      button.addActionListener(new ActionListener() {
        public void actionPerformed(ActionEvent e) {
          System.out.println("Hello There: event received: " + e);
        }
      });
    }
}
```

If we want the button to do something, we have to specify an ActionListener object, which has a single method: actionPerformed. We used an *anonymous inner class* to implement the interface and the method.

It is very common in Java APIs to define custom interfaces like this that declare a single abstract method. They are often labelled "callback methods," because they are typically used to enable registration of client code that will be called for particular events.

The world's Java APIs must have hundreds of one-off, special-purpose interfaces like `ActionListener`. It greatly increases the cognitive load on the developer to learn all of them. You spend a lot of time reading Javadocs or letting your IDE remember for you. We've been told that abstraction is a good thing, right? Well, let's introduce abstractions for all these "function objects"!

First, here is an interface that defines a "function" that takes one argument of type parameter A and returns `void`:

```
package functions;

public interface Function1Void<A> {
  void apply(A a);
}
```

You could call the generic method name anything you want, but I chose `apply` because it is a common name in functional programming, derived from the convention of saying that you "apply" a function to its arguments when you call it.

Now, let's pretend that there is a "functional" version of the Abstract Window Toolkit (AWT), `java.fawt.Component`, with a method `addActionListener` that takes a `Function1Void` object instead of `ActionListener`:

```
package functions;
import java.fawt.*;
import java.fawt.event.*;

class FunctionalHelloButtonApp {
  private final Button button = new Button();

  public FunctionalHelloButtonApp() {
    button.addActionListener(new Function1Void<ActionEvent>() {  // 1
      public void apply(ActionEvent e) {                          // 2
        System.out.println("Hello There: event received: "+e);
      }
    });
  }
}
```

I have indicated the changes with the two comments 1 and 2. Otherwise, the code is identical to the previous example.

You might argue that having a custom type for the argument to `addActionListener` prevents a user from passing an arbitrary and inappropriate object to it. You might also claim that the custom name of the interface and the custom method name help document the API for the reader. Neither argument really holds up.

First, giving abstractions special names does nothing to prevent the user from implementing the wrong thing. As far as documentation is concerned, `addActionListener` must document its expectations (as we'll discuss in "The Liskov Substitution Principle" on page 50). The type parameter for `Function1Void<ActionEvent>` must still appear in `addActionListener` signature. That's another bit of *essential* documentation for the user.

Once the developer is accustomed to using `Function1Void<A>` all over the JDK (in our more perfect world...), it's no longer necessary to learn all the one-off interfaces defined in the library. They are all effectively the same thing; a *function wrapper*.

So, we have introduced a new, highly reusable abstraction. You no longer need to remember the name of the special type you pass to `addActionListener`. It's just the same `Function1Void` that you use "everywhere." You don't need to remember the special name of its method. It's always just `apply`.

It was a revelation for me when I realized how much less I have to learn when I can reuse the same function abstractions in a wide variety of contexts. I no longer care about trivial details like one-off interface names. I only care about what a particular function is supposed to do.

Lambdas and Closures

While we've reduced some of the unnecessary complexity in the JDK (or pretended to do so), the syntax is still very verbose, as we still have to say things like `new Function1Void<ActionEvent>() {...}`. Wouldn't it be great if we could just write an *anonymous function* with just the argument list and the body?

Most programming languages now support this. After years of debate, JDK 8 will introduce a syntax for defining *anonymous functions*, also called *lambdas* (see [Project Lambda] and [Goetz2010]). Here is what the planned syntax looks like:

```
public FunctionalHelloButtonApp() {
  button.addActionListener(
    #{ ActionEvent e -> System.out.println("Hello There: event received: "+e) }
  );
}
```

The `#{...}` expression is the *literal* syntax for lambda expressions. The argument list is to the left of the "arrow" (`->`) and the body of the function is to the right of the arrow. Notice how much boilerplate code this syntax removes!

 The term *lambda* is another term for *anonymous function*. It comes from the use of the Greek lambda symbol λ to represent functions in *lambda calculus*.

For completeness, here is another example function type, one that takes two arguments of types `A1` and `A2`, respectively, and returns a non-void value of type `R`. This example is inspired by the Scala types for anonymous functions:

```
package functions;

public interface Function2<A1, A2, R> {
  R apply(A1 a1, A2 a2);
}
```

Unfortunately, you would need a separate interface for every function "arity" you want (arity is the number of arguments). Actually, it's that number times two; one for the void return case and one for the non-void return case. However, the effort is justified for a widely used concept. Actually, the [Functional Java] project has already done this work for you.

Closures

A *closure* is formed when the body of a function refers to one or more *free variables*, variables that aren't passed in as arguments or defined locally, but are defined in the enclosing scope where the function is defined. The runtime has to "close over" those variables so they are available when the function is actually executed, which could happen long after the original variables have gone out of scope! Java has limited support for closures in inner classes; they can only refer to final variables in the enclosing scope.

Higher-Order Functions

There is a special term for functions that take other functions as arguments or return them as results: *higher-order functions*. Java methods are limited to primitives and objects as arguments and return values, but we can mimic this feature with our Function interfaces.

Higher-order functions are a powerful tool for building abstractions and composing behavior. In Chapter 3, we'll show how higher-order functions allow nearly limitless customization of standard library types, like Lists and Maps, and also promote reusability. In fact, the *combinators* we mentioned at the beginning of this chapter are higher-order functions.

Side-Effect-Free Functions

Another source of complexity, which leads to bugs, are functions that mutate state, e.g., setting values of an object's field or global variables.

In mathematics, functions never have side effects, meaning they are *side-effect-free*. For example, no matter how much work sin(x) has to do, its entire result is returned to the caller. No external state is changed. Note that a real implementation might cache previously calculated values, for efficiency, which would require changing the state of a cache. It's up to the implementer to preserve the side-effect-free external behavior (including thread safety), as seen by users of the function.

Being able to replace a function call for a particular set of parameters with the value it returns is called *referential transparency*. It has a fundamental implication for functions with no side effects; the function and the corresponding return values are really synonymous, as far as the computation is concerned. You can represent the result of calling any such function with a value. Conversely, you can represent any value with a function call!

Side-effect-free functions make excellent building blocks for reuse, since they don't depend on the context in which they run. Compared to functions with side effects, they are also easier to design, comprehend, optimize, and test. Hence, they are less likely to have bugs.

Recursion

Recall that functional programming in its purest form doesn't allow mutable values. That means we can't use mutable loop counters to iterate through a collection! Of course, Java already solves this problem for us with the foreach loop:

```
for (String str: myListOfStrings) {...}
```

which encapsulates the required loop counting. We'll see other iteration approaches in the next chapter, when we discuss operations on functional collections.

The classic functional alternative to an iterative loop is to use *recursion*, where each pass through the function operates on the next item in the collection until a termination point is reached. Recursion is also a natural fit for certain algorithms, such as traversing a tree where each branch is itself a tree.

Consider the following example, where a unit test defines a simple tree type, with a value at each node, and left and right subtrees. The Tree type defines a recursive toString method that walks the tree and builds up a string from each node. After the definition, the unit test declares an instance of the tree and tests that toString works as expected:

```
package functions;
import static org.junit.Assert.*;
import org.junit.Test;

public class RecursionTest {

  static class Tree {
    // public fields for simplicity
    public final Tree left;   // left subtree
    public final Tree right;  // right subtree
    public final int  value;  // value at this node

    public Tree(Tree left, int value, Tree right) {
      this.left  = left;
      this.value = value;
      this.right = right;
    }
```

```java
    public final String toString() {
      String leftStr  = left  == null ? "^" : left.toString();
      String rightStr = right == null ? "^" : right.toString();
      return "(" + leftStr + "-" + value + "-" + rightStr + ")";
    }
  }

  @Test
  public void walkATree() {
    Tree root = new Tree(
      new Tree(
        new Tree(null, 3, null), 2, new Tree(new Tree(null, 5, null), 4, null)),
      1,
      new Tree(
        new Tree(null, 7, null), 6, new Tree(null, 8, null)));

    String expected = "(((^-3-^)-2-((^-5-^)-4-^))-1-((^-7-^)-6-(^-8-^)))";
    assertEquals(expected, root.toString());
  }
}
```

However, each recursion adds a new frame to the stack, which can exceed the stack size for deep recursions. *Tail-call* recursions can be converted to loops, eliminating the extra function call overhead. Unfortunately, the JVM and the Java compiler do not currently perform this optimization.

Lazy vs. Eager Evaluation

Mathematics defines some *infinite* sets, such as the *natural numbers* (all positive integers). They are represented symbolically. Any particular finite subset of values is evaluated only on demand. We call this *lazy evaluation. Eager evaluation* would force us to represent all of the infinite values, which is clearly impossible.

Some languages are lazy by default, while others provide lazy data structures that can be used to represent infinite collections and only compute a subset of values on demand. Here is an example that represents the *natural numbers*:

```java
package math;
import static datastructures2.ListModule.*;

public class NaturalNumbers {
  public static final int ZERO = 0;

  public static int next(int previous) { return previous + 1; }

  public static List<Integer> take(int count) {
    return doTake(emptyList(), count);
  }

  private static List<Integer> doTake(List<Integer> accumulator, int count) {
    if (count == ZERO)
      return accumulator;
```

```
        else
            return doTake(list(next(count - 1), accumulator), count - 1);
    }
}
```

We start with a definition of zero, then use next to compute each natural number from its predecessor. The take(n) method is a pragmatic tool for extracting a fixed subset of the integers. It returns a List of the integers from 1 to n. (The List type shown will be discussed in Chapter 3. It isn't java.util.List.) Note that the helper method doTake is *tail-call recursive*.

We have replaced values, integers in this case, with functions that compute them on demand, an example of the *referential transparency* we discussed earlier. Lazy representation of infinite data structures wouldn't be possible without this feature! Both referential transparency and lazy evaluation require side-effect-free functions and immutable values.

Finally, lazy evaluation is useful for deferring expensive operations until needed or never executing them at all.

Declarative vs. Imperative Programming

Finally, functional programming is *declarative*, like mathematics, where properties and relationships are defined. The runtime figures out how to compute final values. The definition of the factorial function provides an example:

```
factorial(n) = 1                      if n = 1
               n * factorial(n-1)     if n > 1
```

The definition relates the value of factorial(n) to factorial(n-1), a recursive definition. The special case of factorial(1) terminates the recursion.

Object-oriented programming is primarily *imperative*, where we *tell* the computer what specific steps to do.

To better understand the differences, consider this example, which provides a declarative and an imperative implementation of the factorial function:

```
package math;

public class Factorial {

  public static long declarativeFactorial(int n) {
    assert n > 0 : "Argument must be greater than 0";
    if (n == 1) return 1;
    else return n * declarativeFactorial(n-1);
  }

  public static long imperativeFactorial(int n) {
    assert n > 0 : "Argument must be greater than 0";
    long result = 1;
    for (int i = 2; i<= n; i++) {
```

```
      result *= i;
    }
    return result;
  }
}
```

The `declarativeFactorial` method might look "imperative," in the sense that it implements a calculation of factorials, but its structure is more declarative than imperative. I formatted the method to look similar to the definition of factorial.

The `imperativeFactorial` method uses mutable values, the loop counter and the `result` that accumulates the calculated value. The method explicitly implements a particular algorithm. Unlike the declarative version, this method has lots of little mutation steps, making it harder to understand and keep bug free.

Declarative programming is made easier by *lazy evaluation*, because laziness gives the runtime the opportunity to "understand" all the properties and relations, then determine the optimal way to compute values on demand. Like *lazy evaluation*, declarative programming is largely incompatible with mutability and functions with side effects.

Designing Types

Whether you prefer *static* or *dynamic* typing, functional programming has some useful lessons to teach us about good type design. First, all functional languages emphasize the use of core container types, like *lists*, *maps*, *trees*, and *sets* for capturing and transforming data, which we'll explore in Chapter 3. Here, I want to discuss two other benefits of functional thinking about types, enforcing valid values for variables and applying rigor to type design.

What About Nulls?

In a *pure* functional language where values are immutable, each variable must be initialized to a value that can be checked to make sure it is valid. This suggests that we should never allow a variable to reference our old friend, `null`. Null values are a common source of bugs. Tony Hoare, who invented the concept of `null`, has recently called it *The Billion Dollar Mistake* [Hoare2009].

Java's model is to "pretend" there is a `Null` type that is the subtype of all other types in the system. Suppose you have a variable of type `String`. If the value can be `null`, you could also think of the type as actually `StringOrNull`. However, we never think in either terms and that's why we often forget to check for `null`. What's really going on is that we have a variable that can "optionally" hold a value. So, why not explicitly represent this idea in the type system? Consider the following abstract class:

```
package option;

public abstract class Option<T> {
  public abstract boolean hasValue();
```

```
    public abstract T get();

    public T getOrElse(T alternative) {
      return hasValue() == true ? get() : alternative;
    }
  }
```

Option defines a "container" that may have one item of type T or not. The hasValue
method returns true if the container has an item or false if it doesn't. Subclasses will
define this method appropriately. Similarly, the get method returns the item, if there
is one. A variation of this method is the getOrElse method, which will return the
alternative value if the Option doesn't have a value. This is the one method that can
be implemented in this class.

Here is the first subtype, Some:

```
    package option;

    public final class Some<T> extends Option<T> {
      private final T value;

      public Some(T value) { this.value = value; }

      public boolean hasValue() { return true; }

      public T get() { return value; }

      @Override
      public String toString() { return "Some("+value+")"; }

      @Override
      public boolean equals(Object other) {
        if (other == null || other.getClass() != Some.class)
          return false;
        Some<?> that = (Some<?>) other;
        Object thatValue = that.get();
        return value.equals(thatValue);
      }

      @Override
      public int hashCode() { return 37 * value.hashCode(); }
    }
```

A Some instance is used when the Option has a value. So, its hasValue always returns
true and its get method simply returns the value. It also provides conventional
toString, equals, and hashCode methods. I'll explain why Some is declared final in the
next section.

Finally, here is None, the *only other valid subtype* of Option:

```
    package option;

    public final class None<T> extends Option<T> {
      public static class NoneHasNoValue extends RuntimeException {}
```

```java
    public None() {}

    public boolean hasValue() { return false; }

    public T get() { throw new NoneHasNoValue(); }

    @Override
    public String toString() { return "None"; }

    @Override
    public boolean equals(Object other) {
      return (other == null || other.getClass() != None.class) ? false : true;
    }

    @Override
    public int hashCode() { return -1; }
  }
```

A None instance is used when the Option has no value. So, its hasValue always returns false and its get method throws an exception, because there is nothing to get! It also provides toString, equals, and hashCode methods. Since None has no value, *all instances are considered equal!* None is also final.

The following unit test exercises Option, Some, and None:

```java
package  option;

import java.util.*;
import org.junit.*;
import static org.junit.Assert.*;

public class OptionTest {
  private List<Option<String>> names = null;

  @Before
  public void setup() {
    names = new ArrayList<Option<String>>();
    names.add(new Some<String>("Dean"));
    names.add(new None<String>());
    names.add(new Some<String>("Wampler"));
  }

  @Test
  public void getOrElseUsesValueForSomeAndAlternativeForNone() {
    String[] expected = { "Dean", "Unknown!", "Wampler"};;

    System.out.println("*** Using getOrElse:");
    for (int i = 0; i < names.size(); i++) {
      Option<String> name = names.get(i);
      String value = name.getOrElse("Unknown!");
      System.out.println(name + ": " + value);
      assertEquals(expected[i], value);
    }
  }
}
```

```
@Test
public void hasNextWithGetUsesOnlyValuesForSomes() {
  String[] expected = { "Dean", null, "Wampler"};;

  System.out.println("*** Using hasValue:");
  for (int i = 0; i < names.size(); i++) {
    Option<String> name = names.get(i);
    if (name.hasValue()) {
      String value = name.get();
      System.out.println(name + ": " + value);
      assertEquals(expected[i], value);
    }
  }
}

static Option<String> wrap(String s) {
  if (s == null)
    return new None<String>();
  else
    return new Some<String>(s);
}

@Test
public void exampleMethodReturningOption() {
  System.out.println("*** Method that Returns an Option:");
  Option<String> opt1 = wrap("hello!");
  System.out.println("hello! -> "+opt1);
  assertEquals(Some.class, opt1.getClass());
  assertEquals("hello!", opt1.get());

  Option<String> opt2 = wrap(null);
  System.out.println("null -> "+opt2);
  assertEquals(None.class, opt2.getClass());
  assertEquals("str", opt2.getOrElse("str"));
}
}
```

After creating an array of Some and None instances in the setup method, the first test uses getOrElse to extract the value for Some instances, or the "alternative" for None instances. Print statements output each case before the assertion verifies the expected behavior.

The second test shows an alternative way to work with the Options. The hasValue method is called to determine if the Option has a value (that is, if it is a Some instance). Only then is the get method called and the value is output and tested with an assertion.

The final test demonstrates the wrap method defined in the test, which demonstrates how an arbitrary method might return an Option instead of returning another type when the value could be null. In this case, if the input String is null, then a None is returned. Otherwise, the input String is wrapped in a Some.

Here is the output from running the test. The following listing shows just the output from the println calls:

```
*** Using getOrElse:
Some(Dean): Dean
None: Unknown!
Some(Wampler): Wampler
*** Using hasValue:
Some(Dean): Dean
Some(Wampler): Wampler
*** Method that Returns an Option:
hello! -> Some(hello!)
null -> None
```

Look at the method signature for the test's `wrap` method again:

```
static Option<String> wrap(String s) ...
```

What's most interesting about this signature is the return value. *The type tells you that a value may or may not be available.* That is, a value is optional. Furthermore, Java's type safety won't let you "forget" that an option is returned. You must determine if a `Some` was returned and extract the value before calling methods with it, or handle the `None` case. Using `Option` as a return type improves the robustness of your code compared to allowing `null`s and it provides better documentation for users of the code. We are expressing and enforcing the optional availability of a value through the type system.

Algebraic Data Types and Abstract Data Types

In the previous discussion the `Option` interface has only two valid implementing types: `Some` and `None`. Mathematically, `Option` is an *algebraic data type*, which for our purposes means that there can be only a few well-defined types that implement the abstraction [AlgebraicDT]. It also means that there are well-defined rules for transitioning from an instance of one type to another. We'll see a good example of these transitions when we discuss *lists* in Chapter 3.

A similar-sounding (and easy to confuse) concept is the *abstract data type*. This is already familiar from object-oriented programming, where you define an interface for an abstraction and give it well-defined semantics. The abstraction is implemented by one or more types. Usually, *abstract data types* have relatively little *polymorphic behavior*. Instead, the subtypes optimize for different performance criteria, like search speed vs. update speed. Unlike algebraic data types, you might make these concrete classes private and hide them behind a *factory*, which could decide which class to instantiate based on the input arguments, for example.

A good example of an abstract data type is a *map* of key-value pairs. The abstraction tells us how to put new pairs in the map, query for existing pairs, remove pairs, etc.

To compare these two concepts, an *algebraic data type* like `Option` constrains the number of possible subtypes that implement the abstraction. Usually these subtypes are visible to users. In contrast, an *abstract data type* imposes no limit on the possible subtypes, but often those subtypes exist only to support different implementation goals and they may be hidden behind a *factory*.

One final point on *algebraic data types*. Recall that Some and None are final and can't be subtyped. Final types are often considered bad in Java, because you can't subclass them to create special versions for testing. That's really only a problem for types with strong dependencies on other objects that would make testing difficult, like networked services. Well-designed *algebraic data types* should never have such connections, so there is really nothing that would need to be replaced by a test-only derivative.

Exercises

Note: Some of these exercises are difficult.

1. Write unit tests for Function1Void and Function2.
2. Write a method that uses recursion to add a list of numbers.
3. Find some Java code you wrote before that does null checks. Try modifying it to use Option instead.
4. Explore the typing of functions under inheritance. Hint: this exercise anticipates "The Liskov Substitution Principle" on page 50. If you get stuck, see the unit tests for the functions package that is part of the code distribution.

    a. Suppose some method m1 takes a Function1<String,Object> argument. What would happen if you passed an instance f1 of type Function1<Object,Object> to m1? In Java, how could you change the declaration of m1 so that the compiler would allow you to pass f1 to it? Why would that be a valid thing to do, at least from the perspective of "safe typing"?

    b. Considering the same method m1, suppose you wanted to pass a function f2 of type Function1<String,String> to m1? How could you change the declaration of m1 so that the compiler would allows you to pass f2 to it? Why would that be a valid thing to do from the safe typing perspective?

CHAPTER 3

Data Structures and Algorithms

This chapter looks at how the principles of functional programming influence the design of data structures and algorithms. We won't have the space to study either in depth, but we'll learn some universal principles by studying a few important examples.

Functional languages provide a core set of common data structures with *combinator* operations that are very powerful for working with data. Functional algorithms emphasize declarative structure, immutable values, and side-effect-free functions.

This chapter is dense with details and it might be hard to digest on a first reading. However, the ideas discussed here are the basis for functional programming's elegance, conciseness, and composability.

Let's start with an in-depth discussion of lists, followed by a brief discussion of maps.

Lists

The linked list has been the central data structure in functional languages since the days of Lisp (as its name suggests). Don't confuse the following classic definition with Java's built-in `List` type.

As you read this code, keep a few things in mind. First, `List` is an Algebraic Data Type with structural similarities to `Option<T>`. In both cases, a common interface defines the *protocol* of the type, and there are two concrete subtypes, one that represents "empty" and one that represents "non-empty."

Second, despite the similarities of structure, we'll introduce a few more implementation idioms that get us closer to the requirements of a true algebraic data type, such as preventing undesired subtypes:

```
package datastructures;

public class ListModule {
  public static interface List<T> {

    public abstract T       head();
```

```java
    public abstract List<T> tail();
    public abstract boolean isEmpty();
}

public static final class NonEmptyList<T> implements List<T> {

  public T        head()    { return _head; }
  public List<T> tail()     { return _tail; }
  public boolean isEmpty() { return false; }

  protected NonEmptyList(T head, List<T> tail) {
    this._head = head;
    this._tail = tail;
  }

  private final T _head;
  private final List<T> _tail;

  @Override
  public boolean equals(Object other) {
    if (other == null || getClass() != other.getClass())
      return false;
    List<?> that = (List<?>) other;
    return head().equals(that.head()) && tail().equals(that.tail());
  }

  @Override
  public int hashCode() { return 37*(head().hashCode()+tail().hashCode()); }

  @Override
  public String toString() { return "(" + head() + ", " + tail() + ")"; }
}

public static class EmptyListHasNoHead extends RuntimeException {}

public static class EmptyListHasNoTail extends RuntimeException {}

public static final List<? extends Object> EMPTY = new List<Object>() {

  public Object      head()    { throw new EmptyListHasNoHead(); }
  public List<Object> tail()   { throw new EmptyListHasNoTail(); }
  public boolean      isEmpty() { return true; }

  @Override
  public String toString() { return "()"; }
};

/* See the text for an explanation of this code */
@SuppressWarnings(value = "unchecked")
public static <T> List<T> emptyList() {
  return (List<T>) EMPTY; // Dangerous!?
}

public static <T> List<T> list(T head, List<T> tail) {
  return new NonEmptyList<T>(head, tail);
```

```
    }
  }
```

First, we surround everything with a "module", a class named ListModule. This is not strictly necessary, but it provides a place for us to define Factory methods that we'll use as part of the public interface, rather than public constructors. Also, it's convenient to define everything in one file. I'll discuss some other benefits of ListModule below.

Next, we define an interface List<T> that holds items of type T (or subtypes of T). Following convention, a linked list is represented by a head, the left-most element, and a tail, the rest of the list. That is, the tail is itself a List, so the data structure is *recursive*. We'll exploit this feature when implementing methods.

Member functions provide *read-only* access to the head and tail of the list. Hence, Lists will be *immutable*, although we can't prevent the user from modifying the state within a particular list element itself. The isEmpty method is a convenience method to determine if the list has elements or not.

Next we have the class NonEmptyList that represents a list with one or more elements. Because a list is an algebraic data type, we need to control the allowed subtypes of List. Therefore, NonEmptyList is declared final.

Now the head and tail methods are getters for the corresponding fields, which are declared final so they are *immutable*.* We'll retain control over the structure of the list. Hopefully, the user will make the list elements immutable, too.

Because NonEmptyList never represents empty lists, isEmpty always returns false.

Why is the constructor protected? We want to control how lists are constructed, too. We will use static *factory* methods that are defined at the end of ListModule. This is not required, but it lets us use a construction "style" that is similar to the idioms used in functional languages.

The equals and hashCode method are somewhat conventional, but notice that both exploit the recursive structure of Lists. For equals, we compare the heads and then call List.equals on the tails. Similarly, hashCode effectively calls itself on the tail.

Recursion is also used in toString. It calls List.toString again when it formats the tail.

Now let's discuss the representation of empty lists. What should happen if you call head or tail on an empty list? Neither method can return valid values, so we declare two exceptions that will be thrown if head or tail is called on an empty list.

Before we continue, those of you who know the Liskov Substitution Principle (which we'll discuss in Chapter 5) might be crying, "foul!" Our List *abstraction* says that implementers should return valid objects, not throw exceptions. Isn't this a violation of LSP?

---

* We don't care about using JavaBeans conventions for accessors in this case, because that convention doesn't serve a useful purpose here.

After our discussion of the `Option` type in Chapter 2, we better not return `null`! We could change `head` to return `Option<T>` and `tail` to return `Option<List<T>>`. You should try this yourself (see the Exercises for this chapter).

Another approach, however, is to say that the list *type* specifies a protocol that you should never call `head` or `tail` on an empty list. To do so is an "exceptional" condition. If you think about it, you will have to check any list to see if it's empty, one way or the other. You can either call `isEmpty` first and only call `head` or `tail` if it is not empty, or you can use `Option` as the return type and test for when `None` is returned, meaning the list is empty.

This checking may sound tedious, but it sure beats debugging `NullPointerExceptions` in production. Fortunately, you don't need to do these checks very often, as we'll see when we add *combinator* methods to `List` later on.

Back to the implementation. Recall that we defined `None` with a conventional class, even though *all instances of None<T> for all types T are equivalent*, because `None` carries no state information. It is effectively just a "marker" object. Empty lists are the same, stateless and used as list terminators and occasionally on their own. Now, however, we'll really use just one instance, a Singleton object, to represent all empty lists.

`ListModule` declares a static final `List<? extends Object>` named `EMPTY`, an instance of an anonymous inner class. Its `head` and `tail` methods throw the exceptions we described above and its `isEmpty` method always returns true. Note the type parameter, `? extends Object`, which means you could assign any `List<X>` for some `X` to `EMPTY`. This is needed for how we use `EMPTY`, which we'll discuss in a moment. The following sidebar discusses what this type expression means.

No `equals` and `hashCode` methods are required, since there is only one empty list object, the default implementations for `Object` are sufficient. Also, `toString` returns empty parentheses to represent a list of zero elements.

Now we come to the `public static` Factory methods that clients use to instantiate lists, rather than calling constructors directly. Just as there are two concrete types, there are two factory methods, one for each type.

The first static method, `emptyList` "creates" an empty list. In fact, it returns `EMPTY`, but it appears to do something unspeakably evil; it *downcasts* from `List<Object>` to the correct `List<T>` type!

Well, this actually isn't evil, because `EMPTY` carries no state, just like `None`. No `ClassCastExceptions` will ever occur when you use it. So, in practical terms, we are safe and our factory method hides our hack from users. We added the annotation to suppress warnings from the compiler.

Type parameters for generic methods like this are one of the few places where Java uses type inference when you call the method. Java will figure out the appropriate value for `T` from the type of the variable to which you assign the returned value.

The second factory method creates a non-empty list. We call it list to look similar to a constructor. Really, it's effectively just a shorthand way of saying new NonEmpty List<T>(…) with less noise. Even the type parameter is inferred, as you'll see when we discuss the test.

The primary benefit of factories is the way they create an abstraction for construction. Calling new is a form a *strong coupling* and prevents the substitution of instances of different concrete types, depending on the context. As a simple example, the list factory method could determine if an identical list already exists and return it instead. This would be safe since the lists are immutable (ignoring the possibility of mutable list elements).

We can see all this in action by looking at a test, ListTest. It's long, so I'll just show excerpts. For example, we'll omit the equality tests[†]:

```
package datastructures;
import static datastructures.ListModule.*;
...
public class ListTest {
  List<String> EMPTYLS = emptyList(); // The String parameter is inferred!
  List<Long>   EMPTYLL = emptyList();

  @Test(expected = EmptyListHasNoHead.class)
  public void callingHeadOnAnEmptyListRaises() {
    EMPTYLS.head();
  }

  @Test(expected = EmptyListHasNoTail.class)
  public void callingTailOnAnEmptyListRaises() {
    EMPTYLS.tail();
  }

  @Test
```

† The full listing is in the downloadable code examples, test/datastructures/ListTest.java.

```
  public void callingTailOnAListWithMultiplElementsReturnsANonEmptyList() {
    List<String> tail = list("one", list("two", EMPTYLS)).tail();
    assertEquals(list("two", EMPTYLS), tail);
  }

  @Test
  public void callingHeadOnANonEmptyListReturnsTheHead() {
    String head = list("one", EMPTYLS).head();
    assertEquals("one", head);
  }

  @Test
  public void AllEmptyListsAreEqual() {
    assertEquals(EMPTYLS, EMPTYLL);
  }

  @Test
  public void ListsAreRecursiveStructures() {
    List<String> list1 = list("one", list("two", list("three", EMPTYLS)));
    assertEquals("(one, (two, (three, ()))))", list1.toString());
  }
  ...
}
```

The test makes two "different" empty lists, one of type List<String> and one of type List<Long>, using the emptyList factory methods. However, the second to last test verifies that they are actually equal.

The first two tests verify that the appropriate exceptions are thrown if head and tail are called on empty lists. The next two tests verify that the head and tail of non-empty lists can be extracted.

The last test shows the nice recursive-looking representation that toString returns:

```
(one, (two, (three, ())))
```

Recursion is used in ListModule. A successful recursion must eventually terminate. You would have an infinite recursion if loops in a list were possible. The factory methods prevent this as they can only create lists terminated by EMPTY. Hence, the API enforces good behavior.

> *Pure* functional programming uses recursion instead of loops, since a loop counter would have to be mutable.

We used a few idioms to enforce the algebraic data type constraint that the type hierarchy must be closed, with only two concrete types to represent all lists. The final keyword prevents subclassing NonEmptyList and using an anonymous class for EMPTY accomplishes the same goal. However, Java doesn't give us a way to prevent other implementations of the List<T> interface itself, if we want to keep it public.

We are accustomed to saying that instances of a class can only have certain valid states and state transitions. Notice that algebraic data types are making the same kinds of assertions about types themselves, imposing a rigor that helps us think about allowed representations of state and transitions from an instance representing one state to an instance representing another state.

Maps

Let's talk briefly about maps, which associate keys with values, as in this familiar Java example:

```
Map<String,String> languageToType = new HashMap<String,String>();
languageToType.put("Java",    "Object Oriented");
languageToType.put("Ruby",    "Object Oriented");
languageToType.put("Clojure", "Functional");
languageToType.put("Scala" ,  "Hybrid Object-Functional");
```

Maps don't make good *algebraic data types*, because the value of defining an "empty" vs. a "non-empty" type (or similar decomposition) is less useful. In part, this reflects the fact that the "obvious" implementation of List is strongly implied by the head and tail design.

There is no such obvious implementation of Map. In fact, we need flexibility to provide different implementations for different performance goals. Instead, Map is a good example of an *abstract data type* (see "Algebraic Data Types and Abstract Data Types" on page 21).

I'll leave it as an exercise for you to implement a functional-style map (see Exercises). Instead, let's look at operations that work for lists, maps, and other collections.

Combinator Functions: The Collection Power Tools

You already think of lists, maps, etc. as "collections," all with a set of common methods. Most collections support Java Iterators, too. In functional programming, there are three core operations that are the basis of almost all work you do with collections:

Filter
   Create a new collection, keeping only the elements for which a filter method returns true. The size of the new collection will be less than or equal to the size of the original collection.

Map
   Create a new collection where each element from the original collection is transformed into a new value. Both the original collection and the new collection will have the same size. (Not to be confused with the Map data structure.)

Fold

Starting with a "seed" value, traverse through the collection and use each element to build up a new final value where each element from the original collection "contributes" to the final value. An example is summing a list of integers.

Many other common operations can be built on top of these three. Together they are the basis for implementing concise and *composable* behaviors. Let's see how.

Returning to our `ListModule` implementation, let's add these methods (plus one other). Here is version 2 of `ListModule`, where I'll only show what's new to save space[‡]:

```
package datastructures2;
...
public class ListModule {
  public static interface List<T> {
    ...
    public      List<T> filter   (Function1<T,Boolean> f);
    public <T2> List<T2> map      (Function1<T,T2> f);
    public <T2> T2       foldLeft  (T2 seed, Function2<T2,T,T2> f);
    public <T2> T2       foldRight (T2 seed, Function2<T,T2,T2> f);
    public      void     foreach   (Function1Void<T> f);
  }

  public static final class NonEmptyList<T> implements List<T> {
    ...
    public List<T> filter (Function1<T,Boolean> f) {
      if (f.apply(head())) {
        return list(head(), tail().filter(f));
      } else {
        return tail().filter(f);
      }
    }

    public <T2> List<T2> map (Function1<T,T2> f) {
      return list(f.apply(head()), tail().map(f));
    }

    public <T2> T2 foldLeft (T2 seed, Function2<T2,T,T2> f) {
      return tail().foldLeft(f.apply(seed, head()), f);
    }

    public <T2> T2 foldRight (T2 seed, Function2<T,T2,T2> f) {
      return f.apply(head(), tail().foldRight(seed, f));
    }

    public void foreach (Function1Void<T> f) {
      f.apply(head());
      tail().foreach(f);
    }
  }

  public static final List<? extends Object> EMPTY = new List<Object>() {
```

[‡] The full listing is in the downloadable code examples, src/datastructures2/ListModule.java.

```
...
    public      List<Object> filter (Function1<Object,Boolean> f) { return this; }
    public <T2> List<T2>  map (Function1<Object,T2> f) { return emptyList(); }

    public <T2> T2 foldLeft  (T2 seed, Function2<T2,Object,T2> f) { return seed; }
    public <T2> T2 foldRight (T2 seed, Function2<Object,T2,T2> f) { return seed; }

    public void foreach (Function1Void<Object> f) {}
  };
}
```

There are five new methods declared in the List interface. We need two versions of fold, foldLeft and foldRight, for reasons we'll discuss in a moment. Also, I've added a foreach method for convenience.

Each implementation for the five new methods in NonEmptyList is recursive, yet there are no checks for the end of the recursion! The corresponding implementation in EMPTY terminates the recursion. This means we have eliminated the need for conditional tests, replacing them with object-oriented polymorphism!

Recall that the filter method will return a new List. It takes a Function1<T,Boolean> f and applies f to each element. In Empty, filter just returns EMPTY. In NonEmptyList, if the result of applying f to head (f.apply(head())) is true, then filter constructs a new list with head and the result of calling filter on the tail. Otherwise, filter just returns the result of applying filter to the tail, thereby discarding head. So, filter is recursive and it terminates when it is called on an empty list.

The map method is slightly simpler, since it never discards an element. It also uses recursion to traverse the list, applying f to each element and building up a new list with the results. Note that f is now of type Function1<T,T2>, because the goal is to allow the original elements of type T to be transformed into instances of the new type, T2. This time, EMPTY's map method calls emptyList, because it must return an object of type List<T2>, instead of an object of the original type.

The foldLeft and the foldRight methods are the hardest to understand, but they are actually the most important, as all other methods could be implemented using them! We'll start with a general discussion of how these methods work, then return to the implementation details.

The reason there are two versions is because they traverse the collection and apply the function in different orders. In some cases, the ordering doesn't matter. In others, the results will be different. There are other important differences we'll see in a moment.

In a nutshell, foldLeft groups the elements from left to right, while foldRight groups them from right to left. It might help to start with an illustration of how these two methods work. Suppose I have a list of the integers 1 through 4. I want to add them using fold. Consider the following example:

```
List<Integer> listI =
  list(1, list(2, list(3, list(4, emptyList())))));
listI.foldLeft(0, new Function2<Integer, Integer, Integer>() {
```

```
    public Integer apply(Integer seed, Integer item) { return seed + item; }
});
```

Here is how `foldLeft` would add these numbers together:

```
(((((0 + 1) + 2) + 3) + 4) == 10
```

The `seed` of 0 is first added to 1, then the result is added to 2, etc.

Now, here is the `foldRight` version:

```
List<Integer> listI =
  list(1, list(2, list(3, list(4, emptyList()))));
listI.foldRight(0, new Function2<Integer, Integer, Integer>() {
  public Integer apply(Integer item, Integer seed) { return item + seed; }
});
```

Here is how `foldRight` would add these numbers together. The result is:

```
(1 + (2 + (3 + (4 + 0)))) == 10
```

In this case, I exchanged `item` and `seed` in the body of `apply` to be consistent with the output and functional programming conventions.

Notice the similarity between the appearance of how `listI` is declared and how the `foldRight` algorithm is written in the comment. In fact, repeated application of our factory method `list` builds lists in a right-recursive way.

Since addition is associative, the answer is the same in both cases. You would get different answers if you did subtraction, for example.

So, we need two versions of fold because the order matters for non-associative operations. There are two other important differences.

First, imagine that `listI` is actually all positive integers, the *natural numbers*. We showed a simple representation in "Lazy vs. Eager Evaluation" on page 15. The `NaturalNumbers` class has a static value representing zero and the `next` method computes a value from the previous value you pass in.

Now look at the `foldRight` example again. Let's rewrite our previous expression to make it infinite and let's replace the literal numbers with calls to `next` (assuming we did a static import of everything in `NaturalNumbers`). For clarity, I'll first show the expression with the literal numbers:

```
(1          + (2               + (3                      + (...))))
(next(ZERO) + (next(next(ZERO)) + (next(next(next(ZERO))) + (...))))
```

Of course, `ZERO` and `0` are actually equal. `NaturalNumbers` also defines `take(n)`, which returns a `List` of the first n positive integers. Effectively, the recursion in `foldRight` will now terminate when it hits the end of this `List`, as if nested calls to `next` stop after n. If we call `take(3)`, our expression reduces to the following:

```
(1          + (2               + (3                      + 0)))
(next(ZERO) + (next(next(ZERO)) + (next(next(next(ZERO))) + 0)))
```

When the recursion terminates in `foldRight`, it just returns the original seed value of 0.

So, we can see that `foldRight` can be used with infinite data structures, if only the first n elements will be evaluated.

However, `foldRight` has a drawback; it is not *tail recursive*. Why? Notice that we do an addition *after* the recursive call returns. The recursive call isn't the *last thing done*, the *tail* of the algorithm. The *tail-call optimization* can't be applied to `foldRight`.

However, `foldLeft` *is* tail recursive. Let's write the left-recursive version of our last next example:

```
(((0 + 1          ) + 2              ) + 3)
(((0 + next(ZERO)) + next(next(ZERO))) + next(next(next(ZERO))))
```

Recall that `(0 + next(ZERO))`, etc. are recursive calls to `foldLeft`, but the addition now happens *before* the call, to construct the argument passed to the next invocation of `foldLeft`. Hence the recursion is a tail call, the last calculation done.

However, `foldLeft` can't be used for infinite data structures. There is no place where we can replace a call to `next` with the seed, as for `foldRight`. So, `foldLeft` will eagerly evaluate the expression, blowing up on an infinite data structure.

Now let's return to the implementations, starting with `foldLeft`. First, the function `f` is of type `Function2<T2,T,T2>`. The first `T2` type parameter represents the `seed`. Recall that we are building up a new value that could be just about anything; a new list, a String, an Integer (for sums), etc. So, we have to pass a starter or "seed" value. Another conventional name for this argument is `accumulator`, since it will contain the "accumulation" of the work done up to a given point.

The second type parameter `T` for `f` is the type of the elements in the original list. The last type parameter `T2` is the final return type of the call to `foldLeft`. Note that it must be the same as the `seed` type parameter.

`Empty`'s version of `foldLeft` simply returns the `seed`, terminating the recursion. In `Non EmptyList`'s `foldLeft`, `foldLeft` is called on the tail, passing as the new `seed` the result of applying `f` to the input `seed` and `head`.

The implementation of `foldRight` is similar. The `seed` is returned by `Empty`'s version of `foldRight`. However, the version in `NonEmptyList` has key differences compared to its version of `foldLeft`. Note that `f` is applied to the head and the result of the recursive call to `tail().foldRight` *after* the latter has returned. As we discussed above, this is why `foldRight` is not tail recursive.

 Consider these concise and precise definitions: `foldLeft` "is the fundamental list iterator" and `foldRight` "is the fundamental list recursion operator" [Shivers].

To end our discussion of `fold`, note that there is a similar operation called `reduce`, which is like `fold`, but the initial value of the collection is used as the `seed`. Hence, `fold` is more general, because the type of the result doesn't have to be the same as the type of the collection elements. Also, unlike `fold`, `reduce` will fail if used on an empty collection, since there is no "first" value!

Finally, we have `foreach`, the simplest of all these methods. Technically, `foreach` would be disallowed in "pure" functional programming, because it performs only side effects, as it returns `void`! The only useful work that can be done is for the input function `f` to do I/O or other state modifications. For example, you might use `foreach` in a `main` method as the outer loop for all other computations. Here is a contrived example that converts the input `String[] args` to a `List<String>` and then uses `foreach` to print out the list of arguments:

```
package datastructures2;
import datastructures2.ListModule.List;
import static datastructures2.ListModule.*;
import functions.Function1Void;

public class ForeachExample {
  public static void main(String[] args) {
    argsToList(args).foreach(new Function1Void<String>() {
      public void apply(String arg) {
        System.out.println("You entered: "+arg);
      }
    });
  }

  private static List<String> argsToList(String[] args) {
    List<String> result = emptyList();
    for (String arg: args) {
      result = list(arg, result);
    }
    return result;
  }
}
```

Actually, there's a bug here; it prints the arguments in reverse order! (See Exercises).

I said that `filter`, `map` and `fold` are *composable*. All three are methods on `List`, of course. Two of them, `filter` and `map`, return a new `List`, while `fold` can return anything we want. One of our oldest problem-solving techniques is *divide and conquer*, where we decompose a hard problem into smaller, easier problems. We can divide complex computations into pieces using `filter`, `map`, and `fold`, then compose the results together to get the final result.

The following JUnit test shows how we can start with a list of integers, filter them to keep only the even values, multiple each of those by 2, then add them up:

```
package datastructures2;
import org.junit.Test;
import static org.junit.Assert.*;
import functions.*;
import static datastructures2.ListModule.*;
```

```
public class FunctionCombinatorTest {
 @Test
 public void higherOrderFunctionCombinatorExample() {
  List<Integer> listI =
   list(1, list(2, list(3, list(4, list(5, list(6, emptyList())))))));
  Integer sum = listI.filter(new Function1<Integer,Boolean>() {
    public Boolean apply(Integer i) { return i % 2 == 0; }
  })
  .map(new Function1<Integer, Integer>() {
   public Integer apply(Integer i) { return i * 2; }
  })
  .foldLeft(0, new Function2<Integer, Integer, Integer>() {
    public Integer apply(Integer seed, Integer item) { return seed + item; }
  });
  assertEquals(new Integer(24), sum);
 }
}
```

In fact, we call `filter`, `map`, and `fold` *combinators*, because they "combine" with their function arguments and they combine with each other to build more complex computations from simpler pieces. Combinators are arguably *the most reusable constructs we have in programming*.

 The `filter`, `map`, and `fold` functions are *combinators*, composable building blocks that let us construct complex computations from simpler pieces. They are highly *reusable*. The combination of `map` and `reduce` was the inspiration for the *MapReduce* approach to processing massive data sets [Hadoop].

Finally, recall that I implemented these functions using recursion, but code that uses them avoids recursion, as in our `FunctionCombinatorTest` example. That means users of `filter`, `map`, and `fold` don't have the drawbacks of recursion, namely the inefficient stack usage and the potential complexity that can arise in non-trivial recursive functions. We could even reimplement `filter`, `map`, and `fold` to eliminate recursion for better performance. Because these functions are used heavily, we would gain significant performance benefits at the expense of a less elegant implementation, but one that remains hidden behind the abstraction.

That's a lot to digest! Once you're ready for more, see [Bird2010] and [Hutton1999] for more on what these powerful operations can do.

Why Languages Matter

If you venture on to a functional language, like Haskell, Scala, Clojure, or F#, you'll notice that having an anonymous function syntax removes some of the clutter we had to use here. That ease of expression makes it easier to understand the concepts, too.

Persistent Data Structures

It seems that if we want immutable values, we have to make a copy whenever we change a value. While this may be fine for small objects, it will be too expensive for large objects, like long lists and large maps.

Fortunately, we can have both immutability and acceptable performance if we only allocate memory for what is actually changing and we share the unchanged parts with the original object. This approach is called *structure sharing*. Tree data structures provide the balance of performance and space efficiency required to do this. The public abstraction might still be a List, a Map, or another data structure. The tree is only used for the internal storage. Note that the trees themselves and their nodes must be immutable. Otherwise, structure sharing will be dangerous, as mutations through one object will be seen by others that share the same substructure!

To simplify the discussion, let's use unbalanced binary trees. They provide average $O(\log_2(N))$ search times (unless the tree is *really* unbalanced). Real persistent data structures often use one of several 16- or 32-way balanced tree variants to further reduce search times and to optimize other performance goals. We'll skip over these details and we won't cover how you might implement a List, Map, or other object using a tree. However, [Spiewak2011] is an excellent presentation on several widely used persistent data structures (warning: Scala syntax). More technical details can be found in [Okasaki1998] and [Rabhi1999].

Figure 3-1 shows a tree at time "0" referenced as an object named value1.

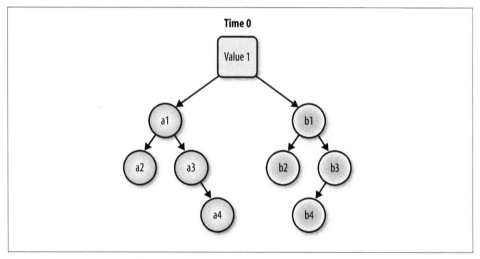

Figure 3-1. Time 0, One Value

Now imagine a user wants to create a new tree that prunes off nodes a1 and its left branch, node a2, but keep node a3 and its right branch, node a4. All we have to do is create a new root node that points to **a3** as its left branch and **b1** as its right branch, as shown in Figure 3-2.

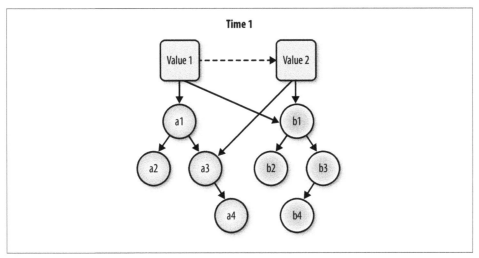

Figure 3-2. Time 1, Two Values, with Shared Substructures

Six of the original 8 nodes are shared by both trees. Only one new node allocation was required, the root node, `value2`.

Note that a *history* of the evolving values is being maintained. We still have `value1` and as long as some code has a reference to it, it won't be garbage collected. This is why these data structures are called *persistent*, not in the database sense (they aren't normally saved to disk), but in the sense that old versions of an evolving structure will remain available as long as needed. We will exploit this feature in "Software Transactional Memory" on page 44.

Some Final Thoughts on Data Structures and Algorithms

From these examples, we can see how immutable values lead us to structure sharing as a way of making new values efficiently, where we share data that isn't changing, rather than make full copies. This can only work if all the data elements are *immutable*. Different kinds of trees are the most useful data structures for *implementing* immutable collection types, because they can be chosen for optimizing various operations, like fast searching for values vs. fast updates.

The use of recursion is also universal, instead of looping. Recursion avoids mutable loop counters and it's a natural fit for recursive data structures, like lists and trees.

However, we can avoid many uses of recursion by using our *combinators*, `filter`, `map`, and `fold`. We can do anything we want with collections using these modular, reusable, and composable functions.

Consider another example, a `List` of email addresses for our customers. We can filter for just the `gmail` addresses. We can map each address in the list to an appropriate anchor tag for displaying in a web page. We can fold over the list to group the users by domain. That is, we can build a map where each domain name is a key and the list of users at that domain is the corresponding value.

In contrast, now imagine that we wrote our own custom `EmailAddresses` class, for example, with one-off methods to do the filtering, mapping, and grouping I just described. We would write a lot more code (and tests) and the special-purpose nature of that code would make the class less attractive for reuse. If we follow this approach with our other domain concepts, we end up with far more code than we really need, with a relatively low density of value per line of code. There would be lots of little ad-hoc types and methods, most of which are seldom invoked and rarely reused.

You might argue that these custom types and methods provide a self-documentation feature. For example, `EmailAddresses.groupUsersByDomain` tells the reader exactly what's going on. That's useful, but there is a better way.

Interest in Domain-Specific Languages is another recent, popular trend (see, for example, [Ghosh2011a] and [Ghosh2011b]). DSLs try to capture the idiomatic language used by domain experts directly in the code. You can implement DSLs in both object-oriented and functional languages. Some languages provide better support for custom DSL syntax than others.

Back to our example, it can be useful to represent a domain with a DSL at the upper levels of abstraction, but questionable to create *explicit* object representations under this surface. We can have a DSL that says, for example `groupUsersByDomain in emailAddresses`, but implement it with `List<EmailAddresses>.foldLeft(new HashMap<…>(), groupingFunction);`, where `groupingFunction` does the "group by" magic on the users and domains.

In "Functional Programming Is More Modular" on page 3, I argued that objects operate at the wrong level of abstraction and they lack a standard set of protocols that are essential for the kind of reuse we want. The core data structures of functional programming and the combinators like `filter`, `map`, and `fold` bring us closer to that ideal.

Exercises

1. Add a factory method to `ListModule` that takes a variable argument list of elements and returns a properly constructed list.

2. Implement a new `ListModule` where `head` and `tail` return `Options`. This eliminates the slight smell of throwing exceptions for the empty list case. However, using `Options` makes some other code more awkward, as a unit test will show.

3. Re-implement the `Option` hierarchy following the idioms used for `List`; e.g., make `None` a static constant.

4. Implement a `MapModule` with an *abstract data type* `Map`. The implementation classes should use side-effect-free functions and immutability. How can you enable the use of alternative implementations that optimize performance and memory usage? What implementations would optimize the following:

   a. A map that contains just a few key-value pairs.

   b. A map that contains a few million key-value pairs.

   c. A map that optimizes insertion performance.

   d. A map that optimizes search performance.

   e. A map that retains the order of insertion (e.g., for subsequent traversal).

5. `ForeachExample` prints the arguments in reverse order. Determine the cause and implement a fix. Hint: consider adding a useful method to `ListHelper` that is commonly found in `List` classes.

6. Reimplement the `equals` and `toString` methods in `NonEmptyList` using `foldLeft` or `foldRight`. Does the choice of `fold` method affect the results?

7. Reimplement the `filter` and `map` methods for `Lists` using `foldLeft` or `foldRight`.

8. Reimplement `foldLeft` and `foldRight` so they don't use recursion. If you use mutable values, preserve thread safety.

CHAPTER 4

Functional Concurrency

Now that we have discussed functional data structures and algorithms, let's return to the topic that has sparked widespread interest in functional programming in the first place: concurrency. Recall this warning from Chapter 1:

Multithreaded programming, requiring synchronized access to shared, *mutable* state, is the *assembly language of concurrency*.

We've already discussed how immutable values make synchronization unnecessary. Yet, mutating state is never completely avoidable. Let's examine two higher-level abstractions that provide "principled" ways to manage mutable state in thread-safe ways: Actors and Software Transactional Memory.

The Actor Model

The Actor model isn't really a functional approach to concurrency, but it fits our general goal of managing state mutation in principled ways. In the Actor model of concurrency, work is coordinated by message passing between "actors." Each actor has a queue, sometimes called a mailbox, for incoming messages. The actor processes each message, one at a time. Carl Hewitt and collaborators developed the actor model almost 40 years ago [Hewitt1973]. [Agha1987] provides a complete description of the theory of actors. Perhaps the best known implementation of actors is found in Erlang, where actors are the core of everything you do in the language.

It's interesting to note that Alan Kay's original vision for objects in Smalltalk is much closer to the actor model than it is to the objects found in most languages [Kay1998]. For Kay, "The big idea is messaging." He also believed that state changes should be encapsulated and not done in an unconstrained way.

This metaphor of passing messages between objects is not only intuitive, it helps clarify boundaries between objects. Have you seen code where one object makes lots of little calls to other objects to get bits of information? How would you change that code if you thought in terms of message passing, instead?

In an actor system, state mutation is handled one of several ways. For some state, it can be the responsibility of one actor to mutate that state. No other code is permitted to do so. When a mutation is required, a message is sent to the actor, which performs all such changes sequentially, thereby avoiding synchronization problems.

A similar model is to allow multiple actors to modify the same state, but only one at a time. A special "semaphore" message is exchanged that tells the receiver that it is safe to modify the state. When finished, the semaphore is sent to another actor.

Both cases run the risk of creating a bottleneck if the scope of responsibility is too large. It might be necessary to break it down into smaller, "isolated" sections.

Fortunately, good actor libraries are available for most languages. Perhaps the best option for Java is the Akka Java API [Akka]. An alternative is also available in [Functional Java].

Here is a simple actor-based program that remembers every string passed to it, keeping the string and the time it was seen in a map:

```java
package actors;
import akka.actor.*;
import static akka.actor.Actors.*;
import java.util.*;

public class AkkaActorExample {
  // server code
  static class MemoryActor extends UntypedActor {
    final Map<String,Date> seen = new HashMap<String,Date>();

    public void onReceive(Object messageObject) {
      String message = messageObject.toString(); // simplifying assumption
      if (message.equals("DUMP")) {
        getContext().replySafe(seen.toString());
      } else {
        Date date = new Date();
        seen.put(message.toString(), date);
        getContext().replySafe("'" + message + "' recorded at " + date);
      }
    }
  }

  public static void main(String[] args) {
    ActorRef remActor = actorOf(MemoryActor.class).start();
    for (String arg: args) {
      // client code
      Object response = remActor.sendRequestReply(arg);
      System.out.println("Reply received: "+response);
    }
    Object response = remActor.sendRequestReply("DUMP");
    System.out.println("Dump of remembered strings: "+response);
    System.exit(0);
```

```
    }
  }
```

For convenience, everything is wrapped in a class, `AkkaActorExample`, which also defines the `main` method. The `MemoryActor` extends Akka's `UntypedActor`, so named because the messages are of type `Object`.

`MemoryActor` implements an `onReceive` method, declared `abstract` by `UntypedActor`, which is called whenever a new message is received by the actor. This handler stores the input message (basically assuming it is a string, for simplicity) and the current time in a *mutable* map. It replies to the caller that the message was recorded.

However, if a special message `DUMP` is received, the actor replies with a "dump" of the current state of the map. Note that the actor manages the *mutable* state and prevents any other code from accessing it. Even the `DUMP` message returns a string, rather than the map itself.

The `main` method uses the Akka idiom for instantiating an actor of instance `MemoryActor` and wrapping it in an `ActorRef`, which is returned to `main`. Akka separates the actor instance from references to it, an example of the Bridge design pattern [GOF1995]. Akka does this so that if an actor instance fails for some reason, it can be restarted without requiring clients to acquire a new reference to the new actor. This is an example of the extensive robustness and error recovery features in Akka's Actor library, which were inspired by similar capabilities in Erlang.

Once `main` has an actor reference, it loops through the input arguments and sends each word, one at a time, to the actor. It then prints the response received. At the end, it sends the `DUMP` message.

To keep the example simple, *synchronous* calls and responses are used, where the code waits for a reply after each message is sent. Normally, you would use asynchronous messages for better scalability, which Akka supports.

If you download the code examples and build the `actor.example` *make* target, it runs this code with the arguments I am a Master Thespian!. Here is the output (omitting some Akka informational messages):

```
Reply received: 'I' recorded at Sat Jun 25 16:14:43 CDT 2011
Reply received: 'am' recorded at Sat Jun 25 16:14:43 CDT 2011
Reply received: 'a' recorded at Sat Jun 25 16:14:43 CDT 2011
Reply received: 'Master' recorded at Sat Jun 25 16:14:43 CDT 2011
Reply received: 'Thespian!' recorded at Sat Jun 25 16:14:43 CDT 2011
Dump of remembered strings: {
  am=Sat Jun 25 16:14:43 CDT 2011,
  a=Sat Jun 25 16:14:43 CDT 2011,
  Master=Sat Jun 25 16:14:43 CDT 2011,
  Thespian!=Sat Jun 25 16:14:43 CDT 2011,
  I=Sat Jun 25 16:14:43 CDT 2011}
```

I wrapped the long line for the "Dump" output. Note that creating the string for the map required iterating through it, which doesn't preserve insertion order, as you would expect.

This example just scratches the surface of what you can do with Akka Actors (as well as other Actor libraries), including distributing actors remotely, managing their life cycles, handling crash recovery, etc. See [Akka] for more details.

Software Transactional Memory

Chances are you've worked on an application with a database backend. A key feature of most relational databases is support for *ACID transactions*, an acronym for *atomicity*, *consistency*, *isolation*, and *durability*.[*] The goal of ACID transactions is to avoid logical inconsistencies in a given set of related records, for example where two simultaneous updates leave the set of records in an inconsistent state, or updates are made that are based on stale data, which could effectively erase more recent updates.

Software Transactional Memory (STM) brings transactions to locations in *memory* that are referenced by variables [STM] (see also [PeytonJones2007]). STM can't provide *durability*, because memory isn't durable (e.g., if the power is lost), but STM can provide the ACI, *atomicity*, *consistency*, and *isolation* in ACID.

The model in STM is to separate references to values from the values themselves. We saw this principle at work in Akka actors. In STM, a program has a reference to a value of interest. The STM framework provides a protocol for changing the value to which the reference "points."

However, values themselves are *not* changed. They remain immutable. Only the references change to point to new values. We saw in "Persistent Data Structures" on page 36 how the appropriate choice of implementation can provide an efficient way to make a new value from a large object without copying the parts of it that aren't changing. Rather, those parts are shared between the old and new version of the object. Persistent Data Structures are exactly what STM needs.

Figure 4-1 shows the state at time "0." There are two references pointing the same value1 of a persistent data structure, adapted from Figure 3-1 in the previous chapter.

Now let's change ref2 to point to a new, updated value, as shown in Figure 4-2.

By time "1," an STM transaction in the context of ref2 has been used to move its reference to value2, which was created from value1, as indicated by the dotted line. Creating value2 does not necessary have to occur within the transaction, just the reassignment of ref2 (but see the example below). Note that ref1 still points to the old value, value1.

---

[*] One of the *big data* trends is to use new kinds of databases that relax this constraint in order to improve throughput and availability.

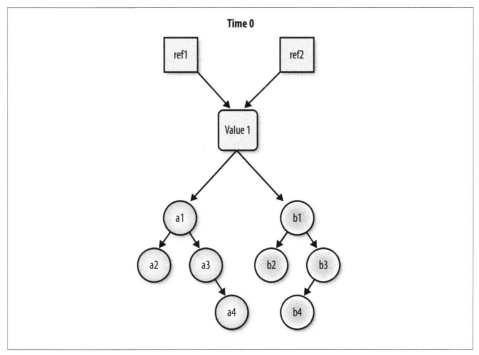

Figure 4-1. Time 0, one value with two references to it

This behavior allows different clients to acquire references to the same value at a particular time, but each can work with the value without fear that it will change unexpectedly, due to the actions of one of the other clients. Recall that a *history* of the evolving values is effectively maintained, as long as there are references pointing to multiple versions. A version with no references will be garbage collected.

So that's how STM works behind the scenes. What's it like for a client to use STM?

There are several STM libraries for Java, many of which are inspired by Clojure's implementation. Akka integrates with the [Multiverse STM]. Below is a simple example adapted from the Akka documentation [Akka]. A reference to an `Integer` value is managed using the techniques described above:

```
// Adapted from Akka example source code.
// Copyright (C) 2009-2011 Scalable Solutions AB <http://scalablesolutions.se>
package stm;
import akka.stm.*;

public class AkkaSTMIntegerCounter {

  private final Ref<Integer> ref = new Ref<Integer>(0);

  public int counter() {
    return new Atomic<Integer>() {
      public Integer atomically() {
```

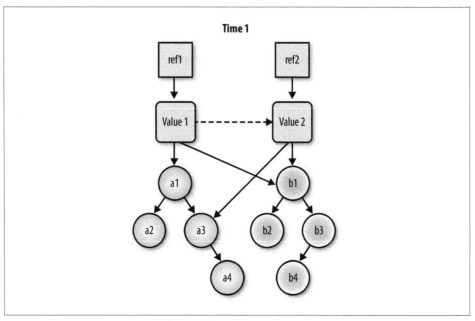

Figure 4-2. Time 1, two values, with one reference to each

```
        int inc = ref.get() + 1;
        ref.set(inc);
        return inc;
      }
    }.execute();
  }

  public static void main(String[] args) {
    AkkaSTMIntegerCounter counterRef = new AkkaSTMIntegerCounter();
    System.out.println(counterRef.counter());   // -> 1
    System.out.println(counterRef.counter());   // -> 2
  }
}
```

First, a typed reference, Ref<Integer>, is created with the initial value of zero. Then, a helper method counter handles incrementing the value and returning the new value. The mutation and update of the reference must be enclosed in an Atomic<Integer> object (analogous to synchronizing a method). The Ref.get method retrieves the *current* value and the Ref.set method sets a new value. Note that wrapping these steps in Atomic prevents updates using potentially stale values from calls to get.

The main method instantiates an AkkaSTMIntegerCounter object, then calls counter twice and prints the results. The numbers 1 and 2 will be printed on separate lines.

For a beautiful exposition on STM, see [PeytonJones2007].

Exercises

1. Using the [Akka] documentation for actors, modify the Actor example to make calls asynchronously. For example, create several actors that send messages to `MemoryActor` and add an actor that `main` uses to receive the replies.

2. Use the Akka/Multiverse API to manage a more complex object, like a collection.

CHAPTER 5

Better Object-Oriented Programming

Now that we have learned about functional programming and its benefits, let's revisit object-oriented programming and see how we can do better with functional ideas.

Imperative, Mutable Code

Recall from "Declarative vs. Imperative Programming" on page 16 that object-oriented programming is primarily *imperative*, where we tell the computer what to do, while functional programming is primarily *declarative*, where we define properties and relations, and let the runtime figure out how to compute what we want. We demonstrated the differences with two versions of the factorial function. The declarative version was clean and simple, while the imperative version was "busy" with mutations, making it harder to understand and prevent bugs. Those problems multiply if your whole code base is like that.

We've seen other reasons to avoid mutability. Mutable objects are not thread-safe by default and it's easy for clients to change their state outside our control. Hence, we should make our objects immutable by removing setter methods and by declaring fields `final`. We should create new instances when the state changes and we should rely on *persistent data structures* for making efficient copies of large collections. We should avoid representing elaborate domain model object "graphs" in memory by limiting the parts of our domain models that we actually implement.

Sometimes we can't avoid mutation. Since Java doesn't perform tail-call optimization, `declarativeFactorial` won't perform as well as `imperativeFactorial`. However, we should choose the *desirable* approach first, then optimize only where *actual* performance data says we should (since our intuitions are seldom correct). If at all possible, we should keep all public abstractions *pure*, even when the internals aren't pure.

Make your objects behave to the outside world as if they are side-effect-free and immutable.

The Liskov Substitution Principle

The Liskov Substitution Principle (LSP; see [LSP] and [Martin2003]) provides the correct way to think about subtyping. Paraphrasing, LSP says that if you have an object of type T1 with a set of *properties*, you can only substitute an object of type T2 if it also conforms to those properties. We say that T2 is a *subtype* of T1. In Java, a *child* class that derives from a *parent* class is considered a subtype.

Subtyping, Inheritance, and Polymorphism

We sometimes think of subtyping and inheritance as the same thing. Inheritance is used for *subtype polymorphism*, where we define type hierarchies with polymorphic behavior. Inheritance is also sometimes used for *implementation inheritance*, a form of reuse, which can cause problems with Liskov substitutability. For completeness, note that Java's generics are an example of *parametric polymorphism*. For example, a List<T> should behave the same whether T is String, Float, etc.

A practical way to ensure that LSP is satisfied is to use Design by Contract [Meyer1997], where you specify allowed properties as one of three kinds of constraints at the level of individual functions or whole types:

- **Precondition:** A condition that must be true when entering the function (or all functions for a type-level precondition). Example: Input parameter x can't be null.

- **Postcondition:** A condition that must be true when leaving the function (or all functions for a type-level postcondition). Example: The return value will never be null.

- **Invariant:** A condition that must be true both before and after the function call (or all functions). Example: Field f will never be null.

If you think carefully about these descriptions, you'll notice that preconditions are requirements on users of the functions, while postconditions are requirements on the functions themselves.

With a Design by Contract tool, these conditions are expressed as executable code. The tool enforces correctness at runtime, such as during testing (see [Meyer1997] and [Contract4J]). These days, Test-Driven Development [TDD] performs a similar role, although it is a less formal approach.

Back to LSP, it can be hard to define *properties* well. The freedom and flexibility of inheritance doesn't provide much guidance, but *design patterns* can help.

Template Method is a pattern that provides a useful constraint on *subtype polymorphism* [GOF1995]. It is error-prone to override concrete methods; it's easy to forget to call the parent method when you should; it's hard to avoid duplication, etc. In Template Method, instead of overriding a concrete method, we implement the method once in the base class as a template that defines the protocol of the behavior. This method calls

---

abstract methods to provide specific pieces of the overall computation. Those abstract methods are implemented in each subclass, giving you a *constrained* form of polymorphic behavior that is easier to keep LSP compliant.

Functional programming gives us a similar tool, *higher-order functions*. Recall that `filter`, `map`, and `fold` implement specific operations, but the details are customizable by the function argument.

 Use Template Method and *higher-order functions* as an aid to conform to the Liskov Substitution Principle.

More on Design Patterns

Some people have claimed that FP makes *design patterns* obsolete, relics of flawed object-oriented languages where missing features had to be retrofitted by coding idioms. This view confuses the concept of patterns with particular example patterns themselves, which may or may not be relevant in different languages. It is true that some of the famous "Gang of Four" patterns [GOF1995] are a standard part of many functional languages. Singleton, Composite, Command, and Iterator might be built into a language or replaced by similar constructs. We just discussed how *higher-order functions* accomplish the same basic goals as Template Method.

At the same time, functional programming has its own set of patterns. One is `fold` and its variants. We'll discuss another one shortly, *pattern matching*.

Many of the functional patterns are named after the concepts from Category Theory that inspired them. You might have heard the word Monad, for example. For our purposes we can say that a Monad is a container with a specific protocol for constructing a new instance of the container using the value in an old instance of the container. Monads have been used to sequence expressions. For example, Haskell code is normally side-effect-free and lazily evaluated. The runtime can defer execution of an expression until needed or never execute it. However, that would not work for IO. So, the "IO Monad" is used to isolate IO actions, maintain their order, and assure that they get executed, while maintaining a clean separation from the rest of the "pure" code.

An ugly pattern that won't be missed is Visitor. It's invasive, it's confusing, and it exposes too many internal implementation details to "visitors." Functional programming gives us other features that are far more elegant for accomplishing the same goals. Let's discuss one of them, *pattern matching*.

Pattern Matching

A goal of Visitor is to replace the need for public getter methods, which expose implementation details. Instead, the visitor is allowed to "go inside the object." A better approach that preserves modularity is to provide a protocol where objects can expose internal values while retaining control over what is exposed and how.

This is one use for *pattern matching* in functional languages (where the word "pattern" is not being used in the design pattern sense). In part, pattern matching is like `switch` statements on steroids, where you aren't limited to checking just for integer or `enum` values (or `booleans` if you use `if` statements).

Functional pattern matching lets you ask questions like "Is this object of type `List`?", "Is this object a list that *starts with* 1 and 2?", etc. For each match, you can specify what action to take.

While you can partially simulate pattern matching with `if` statements in Java, you lose much of the power of the idea without better support. So, I'll use an example written with extensions to Java that are loosely inspired by Scala's syntax, to provide a sense of what's possible. This example matches on an `Object` and looks for `List`s:

```
package datastructures;
// Possible syntax extensions; won't compile for any version of Java.
public class PatternMatchExample {
  public static String match(Object obj) {
    switch (obj) {
      case EMPTY:                    // Is it an empty list?
        return "()";
      case NonEmptyList(1, 2):  // A list with 1 and 2?
        return "(1,(2,()))";
      case List<?> list(head,tail):  // Any other List? Create head, tail variables
        return "("+head+","+match(tail)+")";
      default:                       // Not a List!!
        return "unrecognized object!";
    }
  }
}
```

The `switch` first tests the object to see if it is an empty list. Next, it looks for a two-element list with the literal values 1 and 2. After that, it determines if the object is any `List` at all. Note that if a match occurs in the last case, two variables, `head` and `tail`, are automatically created that reference the *extracted* head and tail of the matched list. Finally, the default clause handles the case of unrecognized types.

Looking at this code, it appears that I broke a cardinal rule of switch statements in object-oriented programming: *Never switch on types in a type hierarchy! Use polymorphism instead!*

I didn't do the wrong thing for two reasons. First, `List` is an *algebraic data type* that will only ever have two concrete classes. So, this switch statement won't break in the future, because we won't modify the class hierarchy. (However, it probably would break if we were using Maps instead, which don't constrain the allowed subtypes.)

The second reason takes us back to Visitor and its primary purpose: to "fake" adding new methods to existing types, where internal access to the implementation is required.

I glossed over the bodies of the clauses just now, but actually, the `match` method is really a `toString` implementation (with some odd parts).

Earlier in the book, I complained about a gigantic `Customer` class that had every possible field and method anyone could want. The better alternative is to limit the methods on any class and to provide a way to implement new behaviors in a modular, *separable* way.

Here's what I mean by *separable*: why do we have `Object.toString` in the first place? It's occasionally useful for debugging, but often we really need XML, JSON (JavaScript Object Notation), or another consistent format. However, it would be crazy to embed XML or JSON dependencies in every object in the system. A better way is to have a module that understands XML serialization and knows how to serialize all the common types to and from XML. It would also need to provide a mechanism for us to specify how to serialize our own types.

The `match` (a.k.a. `toString`) method described above pulls together everything there is to know about converting a `List` to a particular `String` format. We could write similar modules for XML and JSON serialization. We can use the same approach for any behavior that is only needed by some clients, some of the time. When clients need XML serialization, for example, they can import our module for it. When they don't need it, it's not a burden on them.

Pattern matching gives us a new tool for modularity, where we can do data extraction in a way that is controlled by the types themselves. We can use pattern matching to implement new features, yet never pollute the original types with those features. We can localize feature development in one place, rather than spreading it over all the files for a type hierarchy.

 Just because you can join behaviors with state in the same class doesn't mean that you should.

What Makes a Good Type?

When you approach design with a sense of functional rigor, any imprecise type definition becomes suspect. Consider a typical object model that you might see in an IT application, a part of which is shown in the UML diagram in Figure 5-1.

What are the *properties* of the classes in this diagram? How do you ensure that `Man ager` is substitutable for `Employee`, and `401K` (an American tax-deferred retirement savings plan), `Insurance`, and `Tax` are substitutable for `Deduction`?

An object representation of these concepts makes sense conceptually and there is nothing wrong with modeling your domain in objects. However, in software, the imprecision and the fluid nature of real-world objects collides with the precision the machine

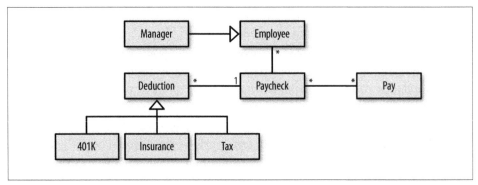

Figure 5-1. UML for an American payroll application.

demands. Worse, even if you find a *snapshot* today of what these concepts mean to you, they will surely change with *tomorrow's* requirements.

Fortunately, not all domain concepts have this problem. Those that are relatively stable and have well-defined properties and operations fit the objectives for types in functional programming.

I think the domain concepts shown in Figure 5-1 don't make good types. Their particular details are fluid, likely to change from one scenario to the next, from one development cycle to the next, even from one team to the next. For these concepts, slice what parts you need into maps of key-value pairs, then implement your scenarios with `filter`, `map`, and `fold`.

However, some of the domain concepts not shown will possess the stable, precise quality that makes them good types. *Money* in the financial world has precise rules for arithmetic and rounding. Post offices have standard formats for *Street Addresses* and there exist databases to verify whether an address is known to exist or not. *Zip Codes* have a standard format and criteria for validity. What examples come to mind from your domain?

In fact, any data that fits in a collection probably should *not* have its own dedicated type. The power of `filter`, `map`, and `fold` compel you! A type wrapper may not justify the cost of developing it.

 Use types to represent domain concepts with stable, clear properties. Consider using maps, lists, trees, and sets to represent other domain concepts that are more fluid and imprecise.

Rethinking Object-Oriented Middleware

In Chapter 1, I discussed my skepticism about Object-Relational Mapping (ORM) and other object-based middleware. They can add needless complexity.

The power of the combinator functions, `filter`, `map`, and `fold`, make a compelling case for keeping data in collections. You can read the data from a database or other service into a collection, transform it as necessary, then send it back to the database, to another service, or to the UI (usually as JSON for web UIs). You avoid the overhead of converting data collections to objects and keep your code simpler. (The *Anorm* API, part of the Play Web Framework's Scala Module, is a good example of this approach to persistence [Anorm].) Having domain objects in your code is nice for understanding the scenario being implemented, but the benefits don't always justify the costs of using them.

Finally, reduction of middleware will increase your team's agility, as more code in a mature application inevitably slows you down.

Exercises

1. Look at a Java application you've worked on recently.
   a. How many classes could be made immutable without much difficulty? How many classes look like feature "kitchen sinks"? How many classes define methods that reinvent operations that would be easy to implement with `filter`, `map`, and `fold`, instead?
   b. How many polymorphic methods don't obey the LSP?
2. Look at the design patterns you use frequently. How might you change or replace them with functional patterns and idioms?
3. Exercise 2 in Chapter 2 explored how functions of different types can be substituted for each other. Can you explain those behaviors using the Liskov Substitution Principle?

CHAPTER 6

Where to Go From Here

Hopefully I've convinced you why functional programming is important for the challenges of our time. We only scratched the surface of this rich field. I hope you'll continue learning and applying functional programming on your own.

So, where should you go next? I find it easier to learn abstract principles by writing real code. You could start by learning one of the scripting languages on the JVM, such as Groovy, JRuby, or Jython. While none of these languages is a functional language, per se, all have many functional features missing in Java, such as anonymous functions, collections with `filter`, `map`, `fold`, and other *higher-order* functions. (The names used by these languages may be different.) Along the way, you'll find these languages useful for general development needs.

However, consider learning a real functional language, where you can see functional programming fully realized. In a few examples in this book we labored to represent some ideas in Java. Functional languages make them much easier to use.

Scala is my personal favorite, because it strives to unify both object-oriented and functional programming. Scala's object-oriented support will let you continue to use familiar object-oriented concepts while you learn and start using functional concepts. Just be careful to avoid the trap of staying in familiar territory! [Wampler2011] provides a brief overview of the language and its compelling features. [Eckel2011] discusses how Scala has the succinct feel of a dynamically-typed language, like Python. For a more in-depth introduction, see *Programming Scala* [Wampler2009], the book I cowrote with Alex Payne. We tried hard to provide a pragmatic, developer-oriented introduction.

Clojure is the other well-known functional language on the JVM. It is a Lisp dialect that offers a powerful vision of how programming should be done, especially the management of state and mutability. In Clojure, all mutations of state are done through specific mechanisms, such as *software transactional memory*. Simple variable assignment is not supported. The greater discipline prevents many bugs and encourages you to think carefully about state and state transformations. Even if you don't like Lisp syntax, it's well worth learning Clojure, as the vision it presents is becoming a major influence on other languages. You can bet that whatever language you are using in

10 years will be heavily influenced by Clojure. *Programming Clojure* [Halloway2009] is an excellent introduction.

Finally, if you're willing to go beyond the JVM, consider learning Haskell, which has been the incubator of many of the leading ideas in functional programming. *Real World Haskell* [O'Sullivan2009] and the whimsically named *Learn You a Haskell for Great Good!* [Lipovaca2011] are great introductions. Haskell is very different than most languages, so patience is required to learn it, but the profound insights it offers reward the effort.

If you are a Windows user, consider learning F#, Microsoft's dialect of OCaml. F# is the first *commercially-supported* functional programming language available. OCaml itself has been used in projects on Wall Street, for example.

There are other great resources for further investigation, many of which are listed in the References. The videos on MSDN's Channel 9, especially those by Erik Meijer, introduce basic and advanced functional topics [Channel 9]. *The Structure and Interpretation of Computer Programs* [Abelson1996] is a classic textbook for computer science. It's not a book on functional programming, per se, but it walks the reader through a logical progression of computing principles, starting with functional programming concepts. Neal Ford's "Functional Thinking" articles provide more examples of using functional concepts in several common languages [Ford2011]. Finally, *Why Functional Programming Matters* [Hughes1990] is a more advanced, yet approachable discussion on the benefits of functional programming.

Functional Tools for Java

There are also good options targeted at the Java programmer. The [Functional Java] APIs define anonymous function types, similar to those we defined in Chapter 2. You can also find various functional data structures, parser combinators, and an Actor library. Similarly, the [Totally Lazy] library offers lots of useful features.

The [Akka] Framework is a powerful, emerging suite of tools for building robust, concurrent applications. Akka includes one of the most performant and feature-complete Actor APIs available. Akka also integrates with many other third-party APIs to provide support for *software transactional memory*, web services, persistence stores, etc. Akka provides both Java and Scala versions of its APIs. I fully expect that Akka will become a widely used tool for JVM-based applications in the next several years, much as the Spring Framework became ubiquitous in the past decade [Spring].

A Recap

In the introduction, I discussed these factors that make me emphasize functional programming over object-oriented programming in my work.

I Have to Be Good at Writing Concurrent Programs
> All of us must know how to write robust code that scales horizontally to multiple CPU cores and servers.

Most Programs Are Just Data Management Problems
> *Big data* requires very efficient management of resources. Those efficiencies also benefit "small data" and "no data" projects. Overreliance on object-relational mapping and other forms of object middleware lead to code bloat, poor performance, and lower agility. We should remember, *What's the simplest thing that could possibly work?* and stay focused on the minimal implementation required. We can express the problem domain through DSLs when appropriate, but we shouldn't assume that our domain object models should be implemented in code.

Functional Programming Is More Modular
> Functional programming moves the abstraction layers lower, to core data structures and *combinator* functions. Combined with immutable values and side-effect-free functions, the modularity and reusability of functional code is usually better than similar object-oriented code. Because objects are so free to expose abstractions any way they want, they are less reusable and composable, which is a paradox.

I Have to Work Faster and Faster
> Functional programming keeps my code concise, by minimizing unnecessary and "one-off" implementation constructs, and it keeps my code logically correct. These qualities, in turn, keep me more agile over the life of the project as requirements change and features evolve.

Functional Programming Is a Return to Simplicity
> Functional programming isn't *simple*, but it represents a return to *simplicity*: the goal of minimizing implementation size and complexity by rethinking our ideas of appropriate design patterns and implementation idioms.

We learned several tools to improve modularity and reuse.

Custom classes aren't always justified
> If data fits in a collection, it probably shouldn't have its own class.

Put your domain in domain-specific languages
> Resist the temptation to faithfully capture your domain model in code. Instead, express your domain in domain-specific languages (DSLs), when useful, and use the most straightforward, concise implementation you can behind the DSL.

Function combinators
> The combinators `filter`, `map`, and `fold` are flexible and composable tools because they are *higher-order functions*. We can exploit that in Java, too, if we standardize on generic `Function` types, rather than rely on one-off, special interface types for callbacks.

Use more generic types, like `Function`

Find ways to replace special purpose types with more general replacements. Really, just be more aggressive about applying the tools you already use to find abstractions that eliminate duplication in your code.

I hope you have found *Functional Programming for Java Developers* stimulating and informative. I hope you are motivated to learn and embrace this exciting trend in software development.

Exercises

1. Look at the [Ninety Nine Problems], originally written for Prolog, and try working out the solutions in Java. It might be easier to use the `ListModule` we discussed in Chapter 3 or the [Functional Java] or [Totally Lazy] libraries. Note that you can find solutions for other languages, too.

References

[Abelson1996] Harold Abelson, Gerald Jay Sussman, and Julie Sussman, *Structure and Interpretation of Computer Programs*, MIT Press, 1996

[AbstractDT] *Abstract Data Types, http://en.wikipedia.org/wiki/Abstract_data_type*

[ACID] *ACID, http://en.wikipedia.org/wiki/ACID*

[Agha1987] Gul Agha, *Actors*, MIT Press, 1987

[Akka] *Akka, http://akka.io/*

[AlgebraicDT] *Algebraic Data Types, http://en.wikipedia.org/wiki/Algebraic_data_type*

[Anorm] *Anorm, SQL Data Access with Play Scala, http://scala.playframework.org/documentation/scala-0.9.1/anorm*

[Baldwin2000] Carliss Baldwin and Kim B. Clark, *Design Rules: The Power of Modularity, Vol. 1*, MIT Press, 2000

[Bird2010] Richard Bird, *Pearls of Functional Algorithm Design*, Cambridge University Press, 2010

[Bloch2008] Joshua Bloch, *Effective Java Second Edition*, Addison-Wesley, 2008

[Caml] *The Caml Language, http://ocaml.inria.fr*

[CategoryTheory] *Category Theory, http://en.wikipedia.org/wiki/Category_theory*

[Channel9] *Channel 9, http://http://channel9.msdn.com/*

[ChurchEncoding] *Church Encoding, http://en.wikipedia.org/wiki/Church_numeral*

[Clojure] *Clojure, http://clojure.org*

[CombinatoryLogic] *CombinatoryLogic, http://en.wikipedia.org/wiki/Combinatory_logic*

[Contract4J] *Contract4J: Design by Contract for Java, http://polyglotprogramming.com/contract4j*

[Eckel2011] Bruce Eckel, *Scala: The Static Language That Feels Dynamic*, *http://www.artima.com/weblogs/viewpost.jsp?thread=328540*

[Erlang] *Erlang Programming Language*, *http://www.erlang.org/*

[Ford2011] Neal Ford, *Functional thinking: Thinking functionally, Part 1*, *http://www.ibm.com/developerworks/java/library/j-ft1/index.html* (first in a series of articles)

[FSharp] *Microsoft F# Developer Center*, *http://msdn.microsoft.com/en-us/fsharp*

[FunctionalJava] *Functional Java*, *http://functionaljava.org*

[Ghosh2011a] Debasish Ghosh, *DSL for the Uninitiated*, *Communications of the ACM*, Vol. 54, No. 7, pages 44–50

[Ghosh2011b] Debasish Ghosh, *DSLs in Action*, Manning Publications, 2011

[Goetz2006] Brian Goetz, et al., *Java Concurrency in Practice*, Pearson Education, 2006

[Goetz2010] Brian Goetz, *State of the Lambda*, *http://cr.openjdk.java.net/~briangoetz/lambda/lambda-state-3.html*

[GOF1995] Erich Gamma, Richard Helm, Ralph Johnson, and John Vlissides ("Gang of Four"), *Design Patterns: Elements of Reusable Object-Oriented Software*, Addison-Wesley, 1995

[Groovy] *Groovy: An agile dynamic language for the Java Platform*, *http://groovy.codehaus.org*

[Hadoop] *Hadoop*, *http://hadoop.apache.org*

[Halloway2009] Stuart Halloway, *Programming Clojure*, Pragmatic Programmers, 2009

[Haskell] *The Haskell Programming Language*, *http://haskell.org*

[Hewitt1973] Carl Hewitt, Peter Bishop, and Richard Steiger, *A Universal Modular Actor Formalism for Artificial Intelligence*, *http://dli.iiit.ac.in/ijcai/IJCAI-73/PDF/027B.pdf*, 1973

[Hoare2009] Tony Hoare, *Null References: The Billion Dollar Mistake*, *http://qconlondon.com/london-2009/speaker/Tony+Hoare*

[Hughes1990] John Hughes, *Why Functional Programming Matters*, *http://www.cs.kent.ac.uk/people/staff/dat/miranda/whyfp90.pdf*

[Hutton1999] Graham Hutton, *A tutorial on the universality and expressiveness of fold*, Journal of Functional Programming 9 (4), Cambridge University Press, July 1999, pages 355–372

[Java6API] *Java Platform SE 6 API*, *http://java.sun.com/javase/6/docs/api/*

[JRuby] *JRuby: 100% Pure-Java Implementation of the Ruby Programming Language*, *http://jruby.org/*

[JUnit] *JUnit, http://junit.org*

[Jython] *The Jython Project, http://jython.org*

[Kay1998] Alan Kay, message on the "squeak-dev" mailing list, *http://lists.squeakfoun dation.org/pipermail/squeak-dev/1998-October/017019.html*

[LazyVsNonStrict] *Lazy vs. non-strict (Haskell.org), http://www.haskell.org/haskell wiki/Lazy_vs._non-strict*

[Lipovaca2011] Miran Lipovaca, *Learn You a Haskell for Great Good!, http://learnyoua haskell.com/*

[Lisp] *Lisp (Programming Language), http://en.wikipedia.org/wiki/Lisp_(programming _language)*

[LSP] *Liskov Substitution Principle, http://en.wikipedia.org/wiki/Liskov_substitution _principle*

[MapReduce] *MapReduce, http://labs.google.com/papers/mapreduce.html*

[Martin2003] Robert C. Martin, *Agile Software Development: Principles, Patterns, and Practices*, Prentice-Hall, 2003

[Mazzola2005] Guerino Mazzola, Gérard Milmeister, and Jody Weissman, *Comprehensive Mathematics for Computer Scientists 2*, Springer, 2005

[Meyer1997] Bertrand Meyer, *Object-Oriented Software Construction (2nd Edition)*, Prentice-Hall, 1997

[Mockito] *Mockito, http://mockito.org/*

[Monad] *Monad (Functional Programming), http://en.wikipedia.org/wiki/Monad_(func tional_programming)*

[MultiverseSTM] *Multiverse STM, http://multiverse.codehaus.org/overview.html*

[NinetyNine] *P-99: Ninety-Nine Prolog Problems, https://sites.google.com/site/prolog site/prolog-problems/*

[OCaml] *Objective Caml, http://en.wikipedia.org/wiki/OCaml*

[Odersky2008] Martin Odersky, Lex Spoon, and Bill Venners, *Programming in Scala*, Artima Press, 2008

[Odersky2009] Martin Odersky, Lex Spoon, and Bill Venners, *How to Write an Equality Method in Java, http://www.artima.com/lejava/articles/equality.html*

[Okasaki1998] Chris Okasaki, *Purely Functional Data Structures*, Cambridge University Press, 1998

[OSullivan2009] Bryan O'Sullivan, John Goerzen, and Don Steward, *Real World Haskell*, O'Reilly Media, 2009

[PeytonJones2007] Simon Peyton Jones, "Beautiful Concurrency," in *Beautiful Code*, Andy Oram and Greg Wilson, editors, O'Reilly Media, 2007

[Pierce1991] Benjamin C. Pierce, *Basic Category Theory for Computer Scientists*, MIT Press, 1991

[ProjectLambda] *Project Lambda: JSR 335 (Lambda Expressions for the Java™ Programming Language), http://openjdk.java.net/projects/lambda/*

[QuickCheck] *Introduction to QuickCheck, http://www.haskell.org/haskellwiki/Introduction_to_QuickCheck*

[Rabhi1999] Fethi Rabhi and Guy Lapalme, *Algorithms: A Functional Programming Approach*, Addison-Wesley, 1999

[Scala] *The Scala Programming Language, http://www.scala-lang.org/*

[Shivers] Olin Shivers, *List Library (for Scheme), http://srfi.schemers.org/srfi-1/srfi-1.html#FoldUnfoldMap*

[Smullyan1982] Raymond Smullyan, *To Mock a Mockingbird*, Oxford, 1982

[Spiewak2008] Daniel Spiewak, *What is Hindley-Milner? (and why is it cool?), http://www.codecommit.com/blog/scala/what-is-hindley-milner-and-why-is-it-cool*

[Spiewak2011] Daniel Spiewak, *Extreme Cleverness, https://github.com/djspiewak/extreme-cleverness*

[Spring] *The Spring Framework, http://www.springsource.org/*

[STM] *Software Transactional Memory, http://en.wikipedia.org/wiki/Software_transactional_memory*

[TDD] *Test-Driven Development, http://en.wikipedia.org/wiki/Test-driven_development*

[TotallyLazy] *Totally Lazy, http://code.google.com/p/totallylazy/*

[TypeInference] *Type inference, http://en.wikipedia.org/wiki/Type_inference*

[Wadler1992] Philip Wadler, *The essence of functional programming, http://citeseerx.ist.psu.edu/viewdoc/summary?doi=10.1.1.38.9516*

[Wadler1995] Philip Wadler, *Monads for functional programming, http://citeseerx.ist.psu.edu/viewdoc/summary?doi=10.1.1.100.9674*

[Wampler2009] Dean Wampler and Alex Payne, *Programming Scala*, O'Reilly Media, 2009

[Wampler2011] Dean Wampler, *The Seductions of Scala, http://polyglotprogramming.com/papers/SeductionsOfScala.pdf*

Glossary

Abstract Data Type

A more formal definition of the familiar idea that types should be defined by abstractions with hidden implementations. An abstract data type is defined only in terms of allowed operations, i.e., without specifying fields, since they are part of the implementation. Abstract data types may or may not be immutable. Representative examples include maps, queues, and stacks, where multiple implementations are possible (including mutable and immutable, as long as all state-changing operations are defined to return a reference to the possibly new instance). Contrast with *algebraic data type*, where only a well-defined set of public subtypes are allowed.

Abstraction

The outwardly visible state, state transformations, and other operations supported by a type. This is separate from the *encapsulated* implementation (fields and methods) of the abstraction. Scala *traits* and *abstract classes* are often used to define abstractions and optionally implement them. *Concrete types* provide complete implementations.

ACID

A desired property of database transactions. They should support atomicity, consistency, isolation, and durability. See [ACID] for more details.

Actor

An autonomous sender and receiver of messages in the *actor model of concurrency*.

Actor Model of Concurrency

A concurrency model where autonomous *actors* coordinate work by exchanging messages. An actor's messages are stored in a *mailbox* until the actor processes them.

Agile and Agile Methods

An umbrella term for several lightweight development processes and specific practices that are designed to minimize process waste, while improving code quality and communications with project stakeholders.

Algebraic Data Type

A special kind of data type that is defined in Java by an interface and a fixed set of possible implementing classes, representing all possible instances of the data type. There may be a well-defined set of operations that maps instances of one type to new instances of the same type or one of the other types. Algebraic data types are always containers for other types (e.g., *list* and *option*). Contrast with *abstract data type*, where the implementing subtypes are not limited and are often hidden from the user of the type.

Anonymous Function

A *value* that is a *function* (as opposed to a class instance or a primitive value) without a name in the usual way that methods are named. Languages that support anonymous functions have a special syntax for defining the value. For example, using the planned *lambda* syntax in Java 8, `addCall back(#{Event e -> log(INFO, e)})` passes an anonymous function to some `addCall` back method. The anonymous function takes a single argument of type `Event` and logs it. Anonymous functions are sometimes called *lambdas* (for historical reasons) or *function literals*. See also *closure*.

Associative Arrays

Another common name for the map data structure, i.e., a collection of key-value pairs.

Base Type

A synonym for *parent type* or *supertype*.

Big Data

A buzzword for the challenges of and approaches to working with data sets that are too big to manage with traditional tools, such as relational databases. So called *NoSQL* databases, clustered data processing tools like *MapReduce*, and other tools are used to gather, store, and analyze such data sets.

Bound Variable

A *variable* that is declared as an argument to an *anonymous function* or is a local variable declared within the function. It is "bound" to a value when the function is invoked.

Bridge

A *design pattern* where a reference to an object is separated from the instance itself, allowing both to vary independently. Also known as "handle/body." Bridge is used in *Software Transactional Memory* to allow references to values to be changed in a controlled way. It is also used in some Actor libraries, like the [Akka] library, to allow clients to keep the same reference to an actor, even if the actual instance has been replaced with a new one.

Category Theory

A branch of mathematics that studies collections of "objects" (used more generally than in object-oriented programming) and "arrows" or "morphisms" that connect the objects in some sense. Category theory has been a fruitful source of ideas for concepts in functional programming.

Child Type or Child Class

A class which is *derived* from another class and also optionally implements one or more interfaces. Also called a *subtype* or *derived type*. See *inheritance*.

Class

A template for creating instances. A class defines implementation of *methods* and *fields*. A class defines *type*.

Closure

A *function* with every *free variable* referenced in the function bound to variables of the same name in the enclosing scope where the function is defined. The free variables are "closed over," hence the name. See also *bound variable*.

Combinators

Functions that return an instance of one of their input types, which can be "combined," according to the rules of *Combinatory Logic*, to build more complex logic. The result can then be applied to values to perform the computation. The `filter`, `map`, and `fold` functions are combinators.

Combinatory Logic

A model of computation invented by Haskell Curry and others that eliminates explicit variables and instead expresses calculations as the combination of operators (*higher-order* functions) that will be applied to data when used.

Composable (or Composition)

The ability to join software "modules" together with relatively little effort to create new behaviors and representations of state from the individual behaviors and states provided by the components.

Comprehensions

"Comprehending" the elements of a collection or *lazy* representation of one (such as all integers), including filtering, mapping, and folding over them. In some languages, comprehensions are syntactic sugar for `fil ter`, `map`, and `fold` invocations.

Concurrency

A model of computation with simultaneous sequences of computation and unpredictable interaction between the sequences. For example, two threads in an application that occasionally communicate. In contrast to *parallelism*, the apparent simultaneity might be an illusion, for example when the program executes on a single CPU with a single core. An example of the unpredictability of concurrency is the handling of asynchronous events, such as user input or network traffic. The precise sequence of execution steps that will occur in the entire program can't be predicted in advance. Contrast with *parallelism*.

Contract

The protocol and requirements that exist between a module (e.g., class, object, or single method) and clients of the module. More specifically, see *design by contract*.

Coupling

In this context, how closely dependent one "module" is on the details of another. *Strong coupling* between two modules makes the reuse and evolution of either module more difficult. It also becomes harder to substitute one module for another, if both satisfy the same public abstractions. Hence *weak coupling* is generally preferred. *Inheritance* is an example of *strong coupling*.

Currying

Converting an N argument function into a sequence of N functions of one argument, where each function except for the last returns a new function that takes a single argument that returns a new function, etc., until the last function that takes a single argument and returns a value.

Declarative Programming

The quality of many *functional* programs and *domain-specific languages* where the code consists of statements that declare relationships between values, rather than directing the system to take a particular sequence of actions. The underlying runtime can then decide how to "satisfy" the rela-

tionships. Contrast with *imperative programming*.

Derived Type

A synonym for *sub type* and *child type*.

Design by Contract

An approach to class and module design invented by Bertrand Meyer for the Eiffel language [Meyer1997]. For each entry point (e.g., method call), valid inputs are specified in a programmatic way, so they can be validated during testing. These specifications are called *preconditions*. Similarly, assuming the preconditions are satisfied, specifications on the guaranteed results are called *postconditions* and are also specified in an executable way. *Invariants* can also be specified that should be true on entry and on exit.

Design Pattern

A solution to a problem in a context. A code idiom or design structure that satisfies the needs of a frequently occurring problem, constraint, requirement, etc. The "context" portion of the definition is important, as it specifies conditions when the pattern is an appropriate choice and when it isn't.

Domain-Specific Language

A custom programming language that resembles the terms, idioms, and expressions of a particular domain. An *internal* DSL is an idiomatic form of a general-purpose programming language. That is, no special-purpose parser is required for the language. Instead, DSL code is written in the general-purpose language and parsed just like any other code. An *external* DSL is a language with its own grammar and parser. In Java, good examples of internal DSLs include most "mocking" frameworks for testing. See, for example, [Mockito].

Eager Evaluation

Evaluation of an expression (such as computing a value) as soon as the expression is encountered, rather than delaying evaluation until the result is actually needed, on demand, which is called *lazy evaluation*.

Eager evaluation is sometimes called "call by name."

Encapsulation

Restricting the visibility of members of a type so they are not visible to clients of the type when they shouldn't be. This is a way of exposing only the *abstraction* supported by the type, while hiding implementation details, which prevents unwanted access to them from clients and keeps the *abstraction* exposed by the type consistent and minimal.

Event

The notification of a state change in *event-based concurrency*.

Event-Based Concurrency

A form of concurrency where events are used to signal important state changes and handlers are used to respond to the events.

Factory

A general term for several related *design patterns* that abstract the process of constructing objects.

Field

A variable in an object that holds part of the object's state.

Final

Keyword for declarations. For types, `final` prevents users from subclassing the type. For methods, `final` prevents users from overriding the members. For variables, `final` prevents users from reassigning the values.

First-Class Value

An indication that the applicable "concept" is a first-class construct in the language, meaning you can assign instances to variables, pass them as function parameters, and return them from functions. In Java, primitives and objects are first-class values, while *functions* and classes themselves are not. Most other programming languages support functions as first-class values, at least in some form.

Free Variable

A *variable* that is referenced in an *anonymous function*, but is not passed in as an argument nor declared as a local variable. Therefore, it must be "bound" to a defined variable of the same name in the scope where the anonymous function is defined, to form a *closure*.

Function

Similar to a *method*, but not bound to a particular class or object. Functions are *first-class values* in functional programming languages, and they can usually be defined "anonymously"; see *anonymous function*. Functions also have no side effects in functional programming, meaning they don't change state, but only return new values.

Function Literal

A less commonly used name for an *anonymous function*. See also *lambda*.

Functional Programming

A form of programming that follows the mathematical principles for function and variable behaviors. Mathematical functions are *side-effect-free* and *first-class values*. Variables are assigned once, so values are *immutable*.

Generics

Types that are defined with type parameters representing other types that they use. For example, Java's List<T>. When an instance of a generic type is created, the type parameters must be specified with actual types. The term *parameterized types* is sometimes used instead.

Higher-Order Functions

Functions that take other functions as arguments or return a function value.

Immutable Value

A value that can't be changed after it has been initialized. Contrast with *mutable value*.

Imperative Programming

The quality of many *object-oriented* and "procedural" programs where the code consists of statements directing the system to take a particular sequence of actions. Contrast with *declarative programming*.

Infinite Data Structure

A data structure that represents a non-terminating collection of values (such as the non-negative integers), but which is capable of doing so without exhausting system resources. The values are not computed until the data structure is asked to produce them. As long as only a finite subset of the values are requested, resource exhaustion is avoided.

Inheritance

A *strong coupling* between one class or interface and another. The inheriting (*derived*) class or interface incorporates the members of the *parent* class or interface, as if they were defined within the derivative. Hence, inheritance is a form of reuse. The derivative may override inherited members (unless declared `final`). For a properly defined derived type, instances of it are *substitutable* for instances of the parent, satisfying the *Liskov Substitution Principle*.

Instance

Another term for an *object* created by invoking a *class* constructor or a value of a primitive type.

Invariance and Invariant

In the context of *design by contract*, an assertion that should be true before and after a method is executed.

Lambda

In the days when Alonzo Church and others were developing *lambda calculus*, it got its name from the use of the Greek letter lambda (λ) to represent a function. As a result, the term is often used for *anonymous functions*.

Lazy Evaluation and Laziness

A feature of mathematics and many functional languages where expression evaluation is delayed until its value is needed, rather than doing the evaluation *eagerly*. This feature is useful for delaying or elimi-

nating expensive evaluations, preventing unnecessary re-evaluations (e.g., through *memoization*), and for representing infinitely large data structures, where only some of the values will be needed. Compare with *eager evaluation* and contrast with *strict reduction*. Lazy evaluation is sometimes called "call by need."

List

The fundamental data structure in functional programming, representing a linked list, which is implemented as a "head" element and a "tail" linked list that represents the rest of the list. Lists are *algebraic data types*; there are only two concrete types that represent all lists, a type for empty lists and a type for non-empty lists. There are also well-defined rules for transitioning from one to the other. Compare with *map*.

Liskov Substitution Principle

Named after its inventor, Barbara Liskov, it specifies that if a type T has certain properties P, then instances of a different type T2 can be substituted for instances of T if and only if T2 also satisfies the same properties P. In object-oriented programming, inheritance is normally used to define these type relationships. See also [LSP].

Map

The common data structure in programming, representing a collection of key-value pairs. Maps have a well-defined abstraction that declares operations that can be performed on the map. A wide variety of implementations are possible, often based on performance and resource tradeoffs. Because there is no fixed set of possible implementing types and the focus is instead on the abstract "specification," maps are an example of an *abstract data type*. Compare with *list*.

MapReduce

A divide and conquer strategy for processing large data sets in parallel. In the "map" phase, the data sets are subdivided. The desired computation is performed on each subset. The "reduce" phase combines the results of the subset calculations into a final result. MapReduce frameworks handle the details of managing the operations and the nodes they run on, including restarting operations that fail for some reason. The user of the framework only has to write the code for mapping and reducing the data sets.

Member

A generic term for a *field* or *method* declared in a *class*.

Memoization

A form of caching that optimizes function invocations. The results from a function's invocations are saved so that when repeated invocations are made with the same inputs, the cached results can be returned instead of re-invoking the function. Memoization is only useful for functions that are *side-effect-free*.

Message

In the *actor model of concurrency*, messages are exchanged between actors to coordinate their work. In object-oriented programming, method invocation is sometimes referred to as "sending a message to an object," especially in certain languages (for example, Smalltalk).

Method

A *function* that is defined by a class and can only be invoked in the context of the class or one of its instances.

Monad

A *Category Theory* concept adopted in functional programming. A monad is a kind of container with a protocol for adding elements to it. For example, Monads are used to sequence computations that must be evaluated in a particular order (such as IO) that would otherwise be lazy and evaluated in arbitrary order, if at all. Monads are also useful for isolating code with side effects (which is also incompatible with laziness).

Mutable Value

A value that can be changed after it has been initialized. Contrast with *immutable value*.

NoSQL

An umbrella term for non-relational data stores, hence the name. These stores sacrifice *ACID* transactions for greater scalability and availability.

Object

A cohesive unit with a particular state, possible state transitions, and behaviors. In Java, an object is an *instance* of a *class*.

Object-Oriented Programming

A form of *imperative* programming that encapsulates state values and related operations, exposing a cohesive abstraction to clients of the object while hiding internal implementation details. Java's object model is based on *classes*; objects are instantiated from classes. Most class-based, object-oriented languages also support subtyping to define specializations and "family" relationships between types.

Overloaded Functions

Two or more functions defined in the same scope (e.g., as methods in a type or as "bare" functions) that have the same name, but different *signatures*.

Overridden Functions

When a function with a particular signature in a *parent class* is redefined in a *child class*, so its behavior changes. Overridden functions must obey the *Liskov Substitution Principle*.

Parallelism

Computation sequences that happen at the same time, because they are running on separate CPU cores or separate servers. Parallelism is a deterministic model in the sense that sequences are spawned at specific points in the program and the program often waits at another point until all the parallel sequences have finished (called "joining"). Contrast with *concurrency*.

Parameterized Types

An alternative term for *generics*.

Parametric Polymorphism

The property of generic types like List<T> that their behavior is independent of the actual type for T.

Parent Type or Parent Class

A class from which another class is *derived*. Also called a *supertype* or *base type*. See *inheritance*.

Partial Application

A feature of many languages where a function can be invoked with only a subset of its arguments supplied, yielding a new function that takes the remaining arguments. Some languages only permit "curried" functions to be invoked in this way (see *currying*).

Pattern Matching

An advanced form of switch expressions that support matching instances by type and extracting values from those types, e.g., *field* values.

Precondition

An assertion that should be true on entry to a method or other entry point. See *design by contract*.

Postcondition

An assertion that should be true on exit from a method or other boundary point. See *design by contract*.

Primitive Type

The non-object types in Java, e.g., int, long, float, double, and boolean.

Pure

Used in the context of functions to mean that they are *side-effect-free*. See also *referential transparency*.

Recursion

When a function calls itself as part of its computation. A termination condition is required to prevent an infinite recursion. You can also have cycles of recursion between two or more functions. See also *tail-call recursion*.

Referential Transparency

The property of an expression, where it can be replaced with its value without changing the behavior of the code (see *memoization*). This can only be done with *side-effect-free* expressions (e.g., functions) when the inputs are the same.

Scope

A defined boundary of *visibility*, constraining what variables, types and their members are visible within it.

Side-Effect-Free

Functions or expressions that have no side effects, meaning they modify no global or "object" state, only return new values.

Signature

For a *function*, the name, parameter list types, type parameters (for generic functions), and the return value. For a *method*, the signature also includes the type that defines the method.

Singleton

A *design pattern* where a class is implemented in a special way so that only one instance of the type is ever instantiated.

State

As in, "the state of an object," where it means the set of the current values of an object's *fields*. The state of the whole program is the set of all object states and the "value" of the stack.

Static Typing

Analyzing expressions in a program to prove that certain behaviors won't occur, based on an analysis of the values the expressions can produce.

Strict Reduction

A concept similar to *lazy evaluation*, but pertaining to how expressions are reduced to simpler forms. See [Lazy vs. non-strict] for more details.

Strong Coupling

See *coupling*.

Structure Sharing

A technique for efficiently copying large, *immutable* data structures, where the parts that aren't changing are shared between the old and new copies.

Subtype

A synonym for *child type* or *derived type*.

Subtype Polymorphism

The technical term for polymorphic behavior of a type hierarchy implemented using inheritance.

Supertype

A synonym for *parent type* or *base type*.

Tail-Call Recursion

A form of recursion where a function calls itself as the *last* thing it does, i.e., it does no additional computations with the result of the recursive call. Tail-call recursions can be automatically converted to loops, eliminating the overhead of creating a stack frame for each invocation. However, neither the JVM nor the Java compiler currently performs this optimization.

Test Double

A generic term for a special object that substitutes for a "normal" object in a test, e.g., to fake network I/O or do some verifications during execution.

Test-Driven Development

A development discipline where no new functionality is implemented until a test has been written that will fail initially, but pass once the functionality is implemented.

Type

A categorization of allowed states and operations on those states, including transformations from one state to another. In Java, the type of an object is a primitive type or the combination of its declared *class* (explicitly named or anonymous), the specific types used to resolve any parameters when the class is *generic*, and finally, any overridden methods that are defined when the instance is defined.

Type Erasure

A property of the *generics* type model on the JVM. When a type is created from a generic, the information about the specific types substituted for the type parameters is not stored in the byte code and is therefore not available at run time, e.g., through reflection.

Type Inference

Inferring the type of a value based on the context in which it is used, rather than relying on explicit type information attached to the value.

Value

The actual state of an instance, usually in the context of a variable that refers to the instance.

Variable

A named reference to a value. If the variable is declared with the `final` keyword, a new value can't be assigned to the variable. Otherwise, a new value can be assigned to the variable.

Visibility

The *scope* in which a declared *type* or type *member* is visible to other types and members.

Weak Coupling

See *coupling*.

About the Author

Dean Wampler is a principal consultant at Think Big Analytics, where he specializes in "Big Data" problems and tools like Hadoop and Machine Learning. Besides Big Data, he specializes in Scala, the JVM ecosystem, JavaScript, Ruby, functional and object-oriented programming, and Agile methods. Dean is a frequent speaker at industry and academic conferences on these topics. He has a Ph.D. in physics from the University of Washington.

Colophon

The animal on the cover of *Functional Programming for Java Developers* is a pronghorn antelope.

The cover image is from *Johnson's Natural History*. The cover font is Adobe ITC Garamond. The text font is Linotype Birka; the heading font is Adobe Myriad Condensed; and the code font is LucasFont's TheSansMonoCondensed.

Get even more for your money.

Join the O'Reilly Community, and register the O'Reilly books you own. It's free, and you'll get:

- $4.99 ebook upgrade offer
- 40% upgrade offer on O'Reilly print books
- Membership discounts on books and events
- Free lifetime updates to ebooks and videos
- Multiple ebook formats, DRM FREE
- Participation in the O'Reilly community
- Newsletters
- Account management
- 100% Satisfaction Guarantee

Signing up is easy:

1. **Go to: oreilly.com/go/register**
2. **Create an O'Reilly login.**
3. **Provide your address.**
4. **Register your books.**

Note: English-language books only

To order books online:
oreilly.com/store

For questions about products or an order:
orders@oreilly.com

To sign up to get topic-specific email announcements and/or news about upcoming books, conferences, special offers, and new technologies:
elists@oreilly.com

For technical questions about book content:
booktech@oreilly.com

To submit new book proposals to our editors:
proposals@oreilly.com

O'Reilly books are available in multiple DRM-free ebook formats. For more information:
oreilly.com/ebooks

Spreading the knowledge of innovators | oreilly.com

Get even more for your money.

Join the O'Reilly Community, and register the O'Reilly books you own. It's free, and you'll get:

- $4.99 ebook upgrade offer
- 40% upgrade offer on O'Reilly print books
- Membership discounts on books and events
- Free lifetime updates to ebooks and videos
- Multiple ebook formats, DRM FREE
- Participation in the O'Reilly community
- Newsletters
- Account management
- 100% Satisfaction Guarantee

Signing up is easy:

1. **Go to: oreilly.com/go/register**
2. **Create an O'Reilly login.**
3. **Provide your address.**
4. **Register your books.**

Note: English-language books only

To order books online:
oreilly.com/store

For questions about products or an order:
orders@oreilly.com

To sign up to get topic-specific email announcements and/or news about upcoming books, conferences, special offers, and new technologies:
elists@oreilly.com

For technical questions about book content:
booktech@oreilly.com

To submit new book proposals to our editors:
proposals@oreilly.com

O'Reilly books are available in multiple DRM-free ebook formats. For more information:
oreilly.com/ebooks

O'REILLY®

Spreading the knowledge of innovators   oreilly.com

www.ingramcontent.com/pod-product-compliance
Ingram Content Group UK Ltd.
Pitfield, Milton Keynes, MK11 3LW, UK
UKHW030727220525
458817UK00008B/255